Student Teaching and the Law

Student Teaching and the Law

Perry A. Zirkel and Zorka Karanxha

ASSOCIATION OF TEACHER EDUCATORS AND

ROWMAN & LITTLEFIELD EDUCATION

A division of

ROWMAN & LITTLEFIELD PUBLISHERS, INC.
Lanham • New York • Toronto • Plymouth, UK

Published in cooperation with the Association of Teacher Educators (ATE)
Published by Rowman & Littlefield Education
A division of Rowman & Littlefield Publishers, Inc.
A wholly owned subsidiary of The Rowman & Littlefield Publishing Group, Inc.
4501 Forbes Boulevard, Suite 200, Lanham, Maryland 20706
http://www.rowmaneducation.com

Estover Road, Plymouth PL6 7PY, United Kingdom

Copyright © 2009 by Perry A. Zirkel and Zorka Karanxha

All rights reserved. No part of this book may be reproduced in any form or by any electronic or mechanical means, including information storage and retrieval systems, without written permission from the publisher, except by a reviewer who may quote passages in a review.

British Library Cataloguing in Publication Information Available

Library of Congress Cataloging-in-Publication Data

Zirkel, Perry Alan.
  Student teaching and the law / Perry A. Zirkel and Zorka Karanxha.
    p. cm.
  Includes bibliographical references.
  ISBN 978-1-60709-509-5 (cloth : alk. paper) — ISBN 978-1-60709-510-1 (pbk. : alk. paper) — 978-1-60709-511-8 (electronic)
  1. Student teachers—Legal status, laws, etc.—United States. I. Karanxha, Zorka. II. Title.
  KF4190.S8Z57 2009
  344.73'078—dc22
                                     2009031911

Printed in the United States of America

∞^{TM}The paper used in this publication meets the minimum requirements of American National Standard for Information Sciences—Permanence of Paper for Printed Library Materials, ANSI/NISO Z39.48-1992.

TO MAX, NOALEE, NAOMI, AND SAM
TO JOANA AND KRIS

Contents

Foreword	ix
Introduction	xi
Chapter One Legal Primer	1
Chapter Two State Statutory Synthesis	25
Chapter Three Case Law Synthesis	31
References	69
Appendices	
A. State Legislation Chart	73
B. Case Law Chart	79
C. Case Scenarios	85
D. Glossary	93
E. List of Sample Resources	99
Notes	101
Index	103
About the Authors	111

Foreword

By David A. Ritchey, Ph.D., CAE, Executive Director,
Association of Teacher Educators

The sergeant in an old television police show, "Hill Street Blues," would always finish his morning briefing with the words, "Be careful out there." The same warning could apply to everyone involved in teacher preparation, particularly those at the culminating stage of student teaching. For student teachers, because of their unique and ill-defined status, the need to be aware of legal issues is great. The legal complexity extends to the representatives of higher education and elementary/education who participate in this transitional stage between upper-level student and full-fledged teacher. As the authors point out in this book, education litigation has remained relatively stable over the last decade, but cases involving student teachers have increased significantly.

The Association of Teacher Educators is confident *Student Teaching and the Law* will become a fundamental resource for student teachers and their mentors at both the university and K-12 levels. Not only does it "fill a gap" for the first time, as the authors explain in their introduction, but it contains useful and important resources, including a glossary of legal definitions, relevant and concise case law examples, and charts providing information on both litigation and legislation in the different states. It is written in easily understandable text that clarifies the dense and often abstract legalese in so many actual court decisions and pertinent statutes. This volume should be on the desk of every student teacher and mentor.

Increasingly, research is showing the critical role teachers play in educating our nation's youth, and we believe proper preparation is the key to helping teachers become successful. The novice teacher simply cannot gain the tools needed to be successful except through classroom experience, and being aware of the legal implications of their actions is critical to this learning and preparation process. The federal government as well as state and local authorities are recognizing the importance of teacher preparation, and states are moving to ensure that the in-class experience is a key component for any teacher's preparation process. As more and more emphasis is put on the role of the teacher and as more and more effort goes into monitoring student performance, student teachers in particular will need to get up to speed quickly in all areas of their preparation, including their legal literacy. This book, selected by the ATE via its competitive publication selection process, should be required reading for student teachers and for their mentors in both colleges/universities and in school districts.

Based in the Washington area, the Association of Teacher Educators is an individual membership organization devoted solely to the improvement of teacher education both for school-based and post secondary teacher educators. ATE members represent over 700 colleges and universities, over 500 major school systems, and the majority of state departments of education. For questions on ATE and its services and its various publications, visit http://www.ate1.org.

Introduction

Student teaching is the key phase in the preparation of the professional instructional personnel of the nation's schools. Yet, the burgeoning literature of education law lacks a comprehensive and current source specific to student teaching. The purpose of this volume is to fill that gap.

Filling the gap is not an easy matter for three reasons. First, the primary readership is heterogeneous, consisting of student teachers, the higher education faculty who prepare and supervise them, and the cooperating teachers and administrators at their student teaching placements. Second, the student teacher—being central in the readership roles—is a special hybrid, being partially a student in higher education but not with the typical full load of campus classes and partially a teacher in K-12 education but not with the compensation and benefits of a full-fledged employee. Third, student teachers need legal literacy not only for themselves, but also for the students they serve and the colleagues with whom they work.

As a result, the scope of legal information represents—like a Venn diagram with four overlapping circles sharing a common core—legal issues for teachers and students in K-12 education and legal issues for teachers and students in higher education. The special selective slice that is central to this common core consists of the state statutes and the case law specific to student teachers, whether as plaintiffs (i.e., the suing party), defendants, or key third parties. In short, the scope of the volume needs to be a little about a lot, with careful selection and specialization.

To fulfill its special purpose, the volume has three parts. The first part consists of a legal primer designed to provide the basic building blocks that serve as the foundation for the aforementioned common core. The second and central parts consist of two chapters—one providing an illustrative synthesis of the various state laws specific to student teaching and the other comprehensively canvassing the available court decisions specifically concerning student teachers and student teaching. The final part consists of a variety of useful materials in the form of appendices, including charts of relevant statutes and case law; selected case scenarios for the purpose of review and discussion; a glossary of acronyms, abbreviations, and legal terms; and a sampler list of relevant resources.

Chapter 1

Legal Primer

Student teachers and those responsible for their supervision have reason to know a wide but carefully selected gamut of education law. More specifically, due to the hybrid nature of the role of student teachers and the varying institutional arrangements for their coursework and placements, the coverage must bridge the legal rights and responsibilities of both students and teachers; the contexts of both higher education and K–12 schools; and sources of law applicable to both public and private institutions.

Yet, the professional literature largely neglects legal issues for student teachers. For example, in one of the very few available sources, Mead and Underwood (1995) wrote a brief legal primer for student teachers, but they limited their coverage to four areas of purportedly common questions—negligence, student records, academic freedom, and due process. However, they provided no empirical support for the frequency of these issues among student teachers, and they only cited four court decisions, the most recent being in 1983.

Similarly, in her more general but purportedly "complete" source on student teaching, Herschler's (2009) "legal issues" section is largely limited to the dischargeable grounds of immorality, absolutely asserting that student teachers are "automatically . . . held to a much higher moral standard than the majority of others" (Herschler, p. 198) and solely advising to "stay out of legal trouble (p. 199)." Although law is obviously only one of many concerns for student teachers, the problems with such statements are that (1) various jurisdictions have adopted a nexus model that requires a connection to classroom performance, in place of the traditional exemplar model for teacher immorality cases (e.g., DeMitchell, 1997); (2) as the rest of this volume shows, this particular issue is of relatively limited significance in comparison to the variety of other legal concepts that student teachers need to know; and (3) the overall trends in the relevant legal areas support a selective preventive approach rather than such circular legal advice.

In this chapter, we provide an inevitably broad but not deep summary of the key concepts, terms, and sources of law applicable to student teaching, with special attention to the legal issues that have arisen in the case law to date, which is comprehensively canvassed in the third chapter and Appendix B. The second chapter and Appendix A cover the corresponding statutory law specific to student teaching. Appendix C provides case scenarios for discussion and review. Appendix D provides a glossary of the abbreviations, acronyms, and legal terminology referred to in this volume. Appendix E provides a sampling of more detailed law-related resources, with examples ranging from those that address either K–12 and higher education law in general to those that focus more specifically on legal issues for students and teachers. Thus, this monograph is the only one available to date that is comprehensive, current, and specific to student teaching.

Before canvassing the legal territory that intersects at the special experience of student teaching, we need to make clear another foundational overlap—the relationship between law and ethics. Simply put, law represents the requirements that our society has established, whereas ethics represents the standards that the individual has adopted based, in this context, in large part on the professional norms in K–12 and postsecondary education. Put another way, law is a set of rules that may be symbolized by "shall" (even though, more fully, the rules alternatively take the converse forms of "may" and "shall not"), whereas ethics may be thought of in terms of what one "should" do. They are similar but not the same. The differences amount to at least two pertinent distinctions.

First, consider the relationship in a vertical way, with ethics limited to professional norms. Specifically, legal requirements are in the nature of the minimum, whereas professional norms, or what is sometimes referred to "best practice," are at the higher level of the optimum. Student teachers "shall," or must, at least do what is legally required, but they "should" do their best in terms of what is ethically expected. The consequences in terms of civil law at the successive stages of entry, conditions, and completion of student teaching, including dismissal or liability, only extend in a binding way to those ethical obligations incorporated in law.

For example, a cooperating teacher who engaged in sex discrimination of a student teacher—whether in the form of molestation or harassment—may be subject not only to a civil liability suit under Title IX (see the Glossary in Appendix D of this volume) but also loss of licensure from a state professional practices board, which enforces those ethical standards codified in state law.

Second, consider the relationship in a horizontal way, with ethics extending to other sources of personal guidance, including religious and family

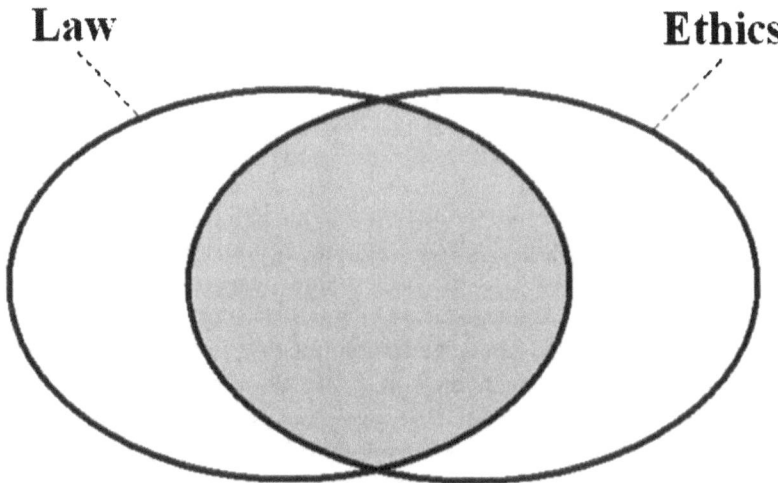

Figure 1.1.

values. Specifically, as illustrated by Figure 1.1, law and ethics overlap, such that many behaviors for student teachers fit as being both legal and ethical; yet, some behaviors may be legal but not—from the point of view of a particular student teacher—ethical, and, conversely, some behaviors may be ethical but not legal.

For example, as the case law in the third chapter shows, a student teacher may choose to exercise strongly held religious beliefs by commission, e.g., evangelizing in the classroom, or by omission, e.g., refusing to follow broad segments of the curriculum contrary to those beliefs. For the particular student teacher, classroom evangelizing would be ethically but not legally appropriate. Similarly, teaching the assigned curriculum, albeit with reasonable and relatively minor adjustment, would be a legal requirement that the student teacher considered unethical. The lack of symmetry is not limited to religious issues. For example, similar quandaries arise when student teachers or their fully professional counterparts, such as special education teachers or school psychologists (e.g., Suppa, Skinner & Zirkel, 1988), engage in advocacy for their students that is beyond the legal protections in federal or state law.

Now, focusing specifically on law, the basic building blocks for this legal primer customized for student teachers start with the sources of law in our federal system of government, which reserves the primary authority for K–12 schools to states. All of the states except Hawaii delegate much of this authority to the local level. However, state and federal governments provide an overlapping framework that—via mandatory, permissive, and prohibitive provisions—establishes legal boundaries and direction for the schools.

The next part of this introduction sets forth the leading examples of laws and legal issues that are of particular pertinence to student teaching.

BASIC SOURCES OF LAW

First, Figure 1.2 illustrates the various sources of law in the United States and their interrelationship. A vertical, one-dimensional view reveals that the constitutional level provides the basic foundation on which legislation and, where authorized by the legislation, regulations successively add more specificity but less strength. Thus, legislation must fit within the boundaries set by the constitution, and regulations must fit within the boundaries set by the enabling legislation; otherwise, these legal rules are *ultra vires*, i.e., unenforceable because they are out of bounds of their underlying authority.

The constitutional level is the most enduring because it is stated in broad, semi-flexible terms, and amendments are purposely difficult. In turn, with successively easier processes, the legislature passes statutes that elaborate the constitutional principles in the form of more specific rules, and administrative agencies adopt regulations that provide even more detailed rules. For example, the Fourteenth Amendment of the U.S. Constitution includes a provision requiring state governments, which include public institutions of higher education and public schools, to provide "equal protection" of the laws, i.e., to avoid illegal discrimination.

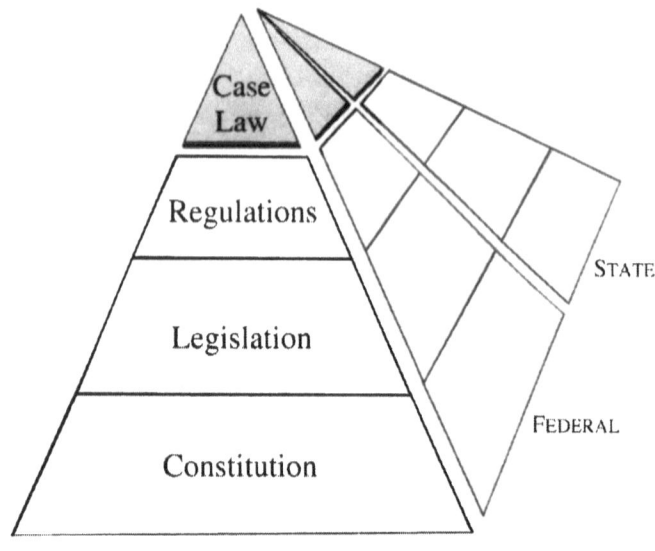

Figure 1.2.

In turn, Congress has enacted various civil rights laws, such as Titles VI and IX, which prohibit race and sex discrimination, respectively, and the U.S. Department of Education has issued regulations that provide more detailed rules in terms of these two types of discrimination in relation to educational institutions, extending—via the Fourteenth Amendment's express authorization for such enforcement—to selected segments of the private sector. Although the administrative agencies, such as the U.S. Department of Education, typically have enforcement mechanisms via compliance reviews and complaint investigations, the major vehicle—or capstone in Figure 1.2—for determining the boundaries for and the meaning of the legislation and regulations is via the courts, which provide a final, litigation level in the form of "case law."

Viewed to take into consideration the added dimension of the successive slices from front to back, Figure 1.2 also reveals that our system of law provides a unifying and uniform federal foundation on which successive state, local sources of law add variety. The dotted line between the state and local slices represents the extension, via partial delegation, of state authority for education to the local level. As a general rule, in the area of overlap under the framework of the U.S. Constitution between the activity of federal and state governments, state law may add to, not subtract from, the uniform foundation that federal law provides. The adding or subtracting is in the direction of the intended beneficiary of the law, such as the student or teacher, individually or as a group; the Constitution's supremacy clause causes federal law to supersede, or trump, state law where they conflict. For example, a state law may add to the federal foundation of Section 504 and the ADA to broaden the definition of disability. Conversely, narrowing the definition would conflict with these federal non-discrimination statutes in terms of their intended beneficiaries, individuals with impairments that substantially limit one or more major life activities. The area of overlap is not overly extensive in the area of K-12 education, because, by virtue of the Tenth Amendment (see Glossary), education is primarily a matter of state law, with the various levels of federal law providing unifying boundaries.

The federal and state sources of law each culminate, for interpretation and application to factual disputes, in their own judicial system. In some cases, depending on the nature and gravity of the claims, these two systems have overlapping jurisdiction. For example, a federal court may litigate a state law claim between litigants of two different states that is beyond a specified jurisdictional minimum amount of damages.

Figure 1.3 shows the three successive levels of the judiciary, which generally are (1) the trial court, (2) the intermediate, appellate court, and (3) the highest court. For the federal judiciary, uniformity is the key characteristic.

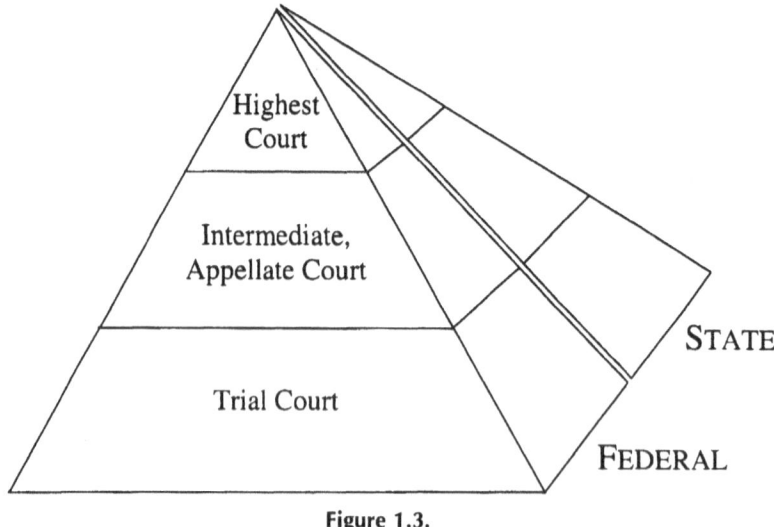

Figure 1.3.

The names (with the abbreviation for case citations) of these federal courts and the official publication (known as "reporter" series)[1] of the decisions for each of these successive levels are as follows:

1. district court ("D.") – "F. Supp." and "F. Supp. 2d"
2. Circuit Court of Appeals ("Cir.") – "F.2d" and "F.3d"
3. Supreme Court – "U.S."

The federal district courts are at the first trial level. Although the number of district courts varies from state to state based on size and population, the total approximates one hundred. The intermediate level consists of 13 federal circuit courts of appeal, with most of them covering a region of several states in one geographic area. One of the two exceptions is the federal court of appeals for the D.C. Circuit, which is limited to the District of Columbia. The other is the court of appeals for the Federal Circuit, which reviews decisions in specialized areas, such as copyright, and from specialized courts, such as the U.S. Tax Court. The top of this pyramid is the U.S. Supreme Court.

The map in Figure 1.4 illustrates not only the boundaries of the various federal circuit courts of appeal but also, albeit indirectly, the concept of precedent. More specifically, a decision by the Third Circuit Court of Appeals, for example, is binding on the federal district courts in Delaware, New Jersey, and Pennsylvania, regardless of which of these states was the origin of the case. Thus, under the doctrine of *stare decisis,* the decision serves as a precedent in the lower courts

Figure 1.4.

within the same jurisdiction, while the same court—in the example, the Third Circuit Court of Appeals—will generally adhere to its earlier decision but may change its mind on occasion. On the other hand, if the U.S. Supreme Court rules otherwise, all of the circuit courts of appeal and the district courts must follow its lead, with the highest court occasionally exercising its discretion to overrule its earlier decision. Thus, in reading the court decisions in Chapter II, be sure to keep the level and jurisdiction of the court in mind.

The same doctrine of precedent applies within the state judiciary, but for nomenclature and the other aspects variety is the key characteristic. For example, the trial levels in Pennsylvania and New York are the Court of Common Pleas and the Supreme Court respectively, whereas their highest courts are called the Supreme Court and the Court of Appeals respectively. In addition to trial courts of general jurisdiction, states have various courts for specialized subjects. For example, family courts handle domestic relations issues, and juvenile courts deal with young persons' conduct that amounts to what for adults are called crimes.

The citations for court decisions generally fit this general template:

Parties' Names / vol.#/publication/p. # (court + year)
Ex. *Ridgewood Bd. of Educ. v. N.E.*, 172 F.3d 238 (3d Cir. 1999)

At the trial level, the sequence of the parties' names starts with the "plaintiff," or suing party, but in appellate decisions—as in the *Ridgewood* example—the first named party is the "appellant," or appealing party, which may be the original plaintiff or defendant, depending on who lost at the trial level. Finally, the appeal to the highest court is typically within the court's discretion to take or refuse. Thus, if the U.S. Supreme Court denies *certiorari*, i.e., declines to accept the case for review, this decision has no precedential effect; the lower court decision remains in effect but does not have the wider binding effect of the Supreme Court.

U.S. CONSTITUTION: LEADING EXAMPLES

Each of the various overlapping and interlocking sources of law includes specific concepts or questions that are significant for student teaching. First, in the federal Constitution, the leading pertinent provisions are the First Amendment expression and religion clauses; the Fourth Amendment search and seizure clause; and the Fourteenth Amendment due process and equal protection clauses.

For each of these powerful but cryptic provisions, the courts are constantly developing interpretations and applications that establish meaning in relation to the current values and issues of our society, including its public schools (e.g., Zirkel, 2001; Zirkel, 2009b). These provisions and, thus, their related "construction" in the courts only apply to public, not private, educational institutions, because these various amendments to the constitution serve as protections for the individual against the government, which is established in the first three articles of the Constitution. Thus, for student teachers, these constitutional claims apply only against school district and public university authorities, not their respective private counterparts.

First Amendment Expression

For First Amendment freedom of expression (see the Glossary), the courts have established different multi-step "tests," or modes of analysis, for public school students and employees respectively. For K-12 students (Zirkel, 2007), the steps include: (1) whether the student has engaged in protected expression (i.e., particularized message and not a threat); and if so, (2) whether the expression is school-sponsored or pro-drug. At that point, the analysis goes down two divergent paths.

On one side, if the court concludes that the answer to question two is yes, school officials only need a rational and legitimate justification to censor or censure the expression, and—given the judicial tendency to defer to public school authorities in such cases—the plaintiff students often lose. On the other side, if the court determines that the answer to question two is no, school officials need a compelling justification, such as proving that they reasonably forecast that the student's expression would result in a substantial disruption of school operations, to win the case. Yet, for students in public postsecondary education institutions, which are the "marketplace of ideas," First Amendment protection tends to be stronger; the substantial disruption standard is the more pervasive standard (*Healy v. James,* 1972).

For public employees (Zirkel, 2006a), the multi-step test starts with the same overall question—whether the employee has engaged in protected expression—but with a different application: a) whether it concerns an issue of public concern, and b) whether it is beyond, rather than part of, the official responsibilities of the employee. If the answer is no to either of these two subparts, the analysis ends in favor of the defendant public employer.

Conversely, if the answer is yes to both subparts, the employee faces three more hurdles in flowchart-like sequence—c) whether the employee's interest in expression as a private citizen outweighs the public employer's interest in operating an efficient educational institution; if so, d) whether the employee's expression was a substantial or motivating action in the public employer's adverse action (e.g., terminating the placement of the student teacher); and, if so, e) whether the public employer would have taken the challenged adverse action regardless of the student teacher's expression.

For student teachers, it is generally more likely that the multi-step test for students applies in First Amendment expression cases, but the choice ultimately depends on whether the expression arose in the school district or public college/university context. This determination depends often but not necessarily on (1) which of these two institutions is the defendant in the case, and (2) whether the student teacher receives a stipend or otherwise fits the role of employee in relation to that defendant. Moreover, these respective multi-step tests are subject to judicial evolution. For example, the Supreme Court added the "pro-drug" part of the student analysis in *Morse v. Frederick,* 2007 and the official-responsibilities part of the employee analysis in *Garcetti v. Ceballos,* 2006. The lower courts are still struggling with the possible extension of *Morse* to other subjects of student expression, such as violence, and the outer limits, if any, of *Garcetti* within the school context, especially for employee expression for teaching or scholarship. Finally, courts sometimes use an alternate criterion in such cases, which is whether the governmental action constitutes viewpoint discrimination.

For example, viewpoint discrimination is often the key to deciding cases of access to school facilities, including but not limited to distribution of religious materials.

When reading in Chapter III the First Amendment cases that have arisen thus far specific to student teaching, bear in mind the date of the case as compared with the current stage of judicial evolution of the applicable analysis. In any event, what all of these rather complicated steps practically mean is that student teachers should think thrice before engaging in controversial expression; the naïve thought that "it's a free country; I can say whatever I want" is a misconception in terms of law.

First Amendment Religion Clauses

Similarly, the two counterbalancing religion clauses—the one prohibiting the Establishment of religion and the one conversely prohibiting the Free Exercise of religion (see the Glossary)—are neither simple nor absolute. The traditional set of criteria for Establishment Clause cases is the so-called tripartite test, which asks—in flowchart-like fashion—these three questions about the challenged governmental policy or activity: (1) whether its purpose is solely religious; if not, (2) whether its effect is primarily secular; and, if so, (3) whether it results in excessive entanglement between church (i.e., religion) and state (here represented by public school officials).

In recent years, occasionally the Supreme Court has used a control/coercion test, which asks whether the defendant public school authorities have effectively controlled the challenged program or activity and whether its implementation has resulted in psychological, if not physical, coercion of students. For example, the Supreme Court held that clergy-led graduation invocations and/or benedictions violated the Establishment Clause (*Lee v. Weisman*, 1992). However, more often in recent years, the Court has used an abbreviated version of the tripartite test that boils down to this primary-effect question: whether a reasonable student observer would view the challenged program or activity as having the endorsement of the public school authorities.

Conversely, the courts have rather consistently used the following multi-step test for Free Exercise clause cases in the public school context: (1) whether the claim of the plaintiff (e.g., student or employee) is based on a genuine religious belief; if so, (2) whether the challenged government policy or activity poses a significant burden on the belief; if so, (3) whether the school has a compelling justification for its challenged policy or activity; and, if so, (4) whether its challenged policy or activity is the least restrictive means to fulfill that justification. However, in recent years, pro-religion plaintiffs have more often relied on First Amendment expression, invoking the viewpoint-discrimination analysis.

The variety of applications of the religion clauses in the education context is mind-boggling, especially given the overlapping roles of students and teachers in K–12 and postsecondary education institutions. For example, just the religion-related case law limited to postsecondary students is extensive and ever expanding (Zirkel, 1999). For the purposes of this monograph, knowing the applicable "test," or sequence of criteria, and the illustrative applications to the limited case law to date specific to student teaching suffices.

Fourth Amendment Search and Seizure

When applying the Fourth Amendment (see the Glossary) to both students and employees in public educational institutions, whether at the K–12 or postsecondary level, the courts have consistently used a balancing test that weighs the individual's reasonable expectation of privacy against the institution's interest in safety. For initiating a search or seizure of a student or an employee, the public institution must have reasonable suspicion, which is less than probable cause. The courts similarly apply a reasonableness standard to the scope or nature of the search or seizure which takes into account multiple factors, such as the gravity of the infraction and the invasiveness of the search or seizure. For exceptional, "special needs" circumstances, where the expectation and invasion of privacy are low and the governmental safety justification is high, the courts have applied the reasonable suspicion standard on a collective rather than individualized basis—for example upholding the constitutionality of metal detectors at the entrance of public schools and of random drug testing of students in extracurricular activities. Conversely, the Supreme Court recently ruled that strip searches of public school students are categorically distinct, requiring individualized reasonable suspicion that is specifically limited to two narrow situations—(1) the items sought present a danger, or (2) the items are concealed in the student's underwear (*Safford Unified School District #1 v. Redding*).

Overlapping with the Fourth Amendment but based on the implicit "penumbra" of various other constitutional provisions as well, courts have recognized a right to privacy for a relatively narrow zone of human activity, which occasionally is triggered in the school context. For example, courts have issued rulings on constitutional privacy in cases concerning K–12 student pregnancy and abortions and in those concerning teacher marital and non-marital intimate activities. Controversial materials and methods in schools sometimes trigger this right of privacy and/or the overlapping parental "liberty" interest under the Fourteenth Amendment's due process clause, which is the next pertinent provision in this overview.

FOURTEENTH AMENDMENT DUE PROCESS

The Fourteenth Amendment provides in part that states may not deprive any person of life, liberty, or property without due process of law. In applying this clause in the context of public education, with school districts and public institutions of higher education being understood to be an extension of "states," the courts have developed both a procedural and substantive side to the overall meaning of "due process" as fundamental fairness.

More specifically, procedural due process means some form of notice and some form of hearing, depending on a balance of individual and institutional interests. However, the courts have interpreted the Fourteenth Amendment as requiring such procedural safeguards if the public educational institution's action has deprived the student or employee of liberty or property. The courts have interpreted "liberty" to mean at its core bodily integrity but extending to severe stigma to one's reputation. They have interpreted "property" in this context to mean a legitimate entitlement or reasonable expectation under state law. Thus, for example, in a pair of cases brought by two respective public university teachers, the Supreme Court concluded that the first one, whose contract was not renewed after one year, did not have a property interest for purposes of procedural due process (*Board of Regents v. Roth,* 1972), whereas the second teacher, who had worked for several years in a system that did not have formal tenure but had policies suggesting equivalent contractual protection, had the requisite property interest if this interpretation was a reasonable one (*Perry v. Sindermann,* 1972).

Correspondingly, for K–12 students, the Supreme Court has ruled that, based on their property interest under state compulsory education laws, suspensions for up to 10 days require school districts to provide at least oral notice of the charges and, if the student protests, an explanation of the evidence and an opportunity to explain his or her side of the story (*Goss v. Lopez,* 1975). Removals of more than 10 days, due to the more serious liberty and property interests, require more formal notice and hearings. Yet, for academic decisions so adverse to postsecondary students as to constitute deprivation of liberty or property, the courts have abstained from requiring a hearing as a matter of Fourteenth Amendment procedural due process, instead finding notice and internal institutional review as sufficient in deference to the expertise of the defendant college or university (*Board of Curators of University of Missouri v. Horowitz,* 1978).

The overlapping concept of substantive due process is even more flexible and favorable to public education institutions. In the K–12 context, courts generally limit substantive due process to institutional actions that are conscience-shocking, i.e., outrageous. Similarly, students in higher education must show that the public college or university's action, at least for academic decisions, is "such a substantial departure from accepted academic norms as to demonstrate that the person or committee responsible did not actually exercise professional judgment" *(Regents of University of Michigan v. Ewing,* 1985, p. 225*).* These institutionally friendly standards reflect not only the modern courts' aversion to the subjectivity of substantive due process but also their deference to educational institution's decision making, particularly for academic issues.

Once again, the applications of this basic framework erected by the Supreme Court in interpreting the due process clause have been extensive, including, for example, a long line of cases concerning the procedural side for suspensions and expulsions of K–12 students (Chouhoud and Zirkel, 2008). Thus, for the building-block purpose of this primer, knowing the applicable sequence of criteria is the key, serving as a foundational framework for obtaining additional pertinent factual information and legal resources.

Fourteenth Amendment Equal Protection

The Fourteenth Amendment also prohibits states from denying to any person the equal protection of the laws. The opposite side of equal protection is discrimination, but the Constitution does not prohibit all governmental discrimination. Rather, because discrimination literally means differentiation, the courts have interpreted the equal protection clause as prohibiting or permitting governmental discrimination in terms of the type of individual interest at issue.

More specifically, if the interest is a fundamental (i.e., constitutional) right, such as free exercise of religion, or a suspect classification, such as race, the courts examine the discriminatory action with "strict scrutiny," requiring the government to show a compelling justification. If, instead, the interest is gender-based, the courts use an intermediate level of scrutiny, requiring a substantial, but not compelling, governmental justification. However, for the vast majority of equal protection cases in the public education context that do not involve any of these specially protected interests, the courts apply a relaxed level of scrutiny, only requiring—with due deference to the defendant educational agency—a rational basis for the challenged action.

Judicial applications of the Fourteenth Amendment equal protection clause in K–12 and postsecondary public education have been numerous, including the Supreme Court's landmark decision in *Brown v. Board of Education* (1954). Of similar significance, the equal protection clause has served as the foundation for several federal civil right statutes.

FEDERAL LEGISLATION AND REGULATIONS: LEADING EXAMPLES

Various federal statutes and their corresponding administrative regulations build in two directions on to the foundation of the foregoing constitutional building blocks, particularly on to the Fourteenth Amendment's equal protection clause. First, they add vertically protections and clarifications beyond the cryptic clauses of the Constitution. Second, they extend horizontally these additions, such that some of these statutes and their regulations apply their limitations to organizations beyond "state," i.e., public, institutions.

For example, with regard to disability discrimination, Section 504 of the Rehabilitation Act of 1973 not only defines "disability"[2] and "discrimination," but also expressly applies to employers, including educational institutions—even parochial schools and religious colleges—that receive federal financial assistance, such as the Department of Agriculture's hot lunch program or the U.S. Department of Education's research, training, and student loan programs. Next, in 1990, Congress passed the Americans with Disabilities Act (ADA), which extended the prohibition of disability discrimination to employers, including private schools not controlled by religious organization, that have 15 or more employees. Finally, in 2008, Congress effectively reversed the intervening stingy judicial interpretations of the meaning of disability under both the ADA and Section 504, making clear in the ADA Amendments that eligibility under these two statutes should be expansive (Zirkel, 2009a).

For each of these statutes, Congress provides the basic provisions by way of legislation. Then, for most of them, the executive branch, via its administrative agencies, issues regulations, or more specific rules—first in proposed form and subsequently, after a review and comment period, in final, binding form. The designated administrative agency also often contributes to the interpretation and enforcement of its regulations via compliance reviews, complaint investigations, and/or administrative adjudications. For example, the U.S. Department of Education's Office for Civil Rights (OCR) administers Section 504 and the ADA in relation to students in K–12 and postsecondary schools, including issuance of not only regulations and policy letters but also implementation of compliance reviews and complaint investigations. Additionally, these students—via their parents when under age 18—have the right to an impartial due process hearing, which generally—under the "exhaustion (see Glossary) doctrine"—must be exercised before proceeding to court.

The courts play a two-fold role upon challenges to or under one or more of these statutory frameworks. First, as illustrated by the contours of Figure 1.2, they determine, upon proper challenge by litigants, whether the legislation is within the boundaries of the Constitution, i.e., is constitutional, and whether the regulations fit within the boundaries of the enabling legislation. Second and much more frequently, after finding what the "facts" of the case are, the courts interpret and apply the pertinent provisions of the legislation or regulations to said factual situation. In these statutory interpretation cases, the courts endeavor to determine Congressional intent based primarily on the statute's language and "legislative history," i.e., recorded proceedings in the committees and two chambers of Congress.

The panoply of federal statutes and regulations, along with the judicial interpretation of them, continues to change in accordance with the evolving values and circumstances of our society. Moreover, each of them has detailed provisions that are not necessarily the same for K–12 institutions as they are for postsecondary institutions.

With the foregoing caveats, Table 1.1 provides an overview sampling of the federal statutes and regulations that apply to students and employees—and thus student teachers—in the educational institutions. The statutes are listed on the left-hand side of the table in their shortened form—e.g., "§ 504" for Section 504 of the Rehabilitation Act and "ADA" for the Americans with Disabilities Act.[3] The column headings identify the specialized interest that the legislation and its regulations target, such as race or gender. The entries in the cells within each column show whether the coverage extends to students ("S"), employees ("E"), or both ("S, E"). Whether the entry is in bold or regular font respectively designates whether said statute tends to be primary or secondary in terms of its frequency—as approximately estimated in terms of the amount of administrative agency enforcement activity and court cases.

As Table 1.1 reveals, the federal statutory scheme that provides individual protections for students and employees in K–12 and higher education extends across a wide range of identified interests. This broad overview does not show the substantial variance in breadth and depth of each statute. For example, several of them have not only extensive statutory provisions but also accompanying administrative regulations. Such a brief overview also does not show the springboard effect of some of these statutes in terms of

Table 1. Framework of Federal Legislation/Regulations Applicable to Students ("S") and Employees ("E")

	Race/ National Origin	Gender	Religion	Age	Disability	Child/ Spouse/Parent	Privacy
Title VI	S						
Title VII	E	E	E				
PDA		E (pregnancy only)					
Title IX		E, S					
EPA		E (pay only)					
EAA			S (access in sec. ed. only)				
ADEA				E			
§ 504/ADA					S, E		
FMLA						E (birth, adoption, or serious illness)	
FERPA							S (records only)

resulting education litigation. The recent long lines of litigation under Title IX for employee-on-student and student-on-student sexual harassment serve as a prime example. Finally, the FERPA entry warrants an additional clarification and limitation. The clarification is that other federal statutes, including the Protection of Pupil Rights Amendment (PPRA) and the Health Insurance Portability and Accountability Act (HIPAA), provide additional, but more limited in the school context, privacy protections for students and employees respectively. The limitation is that the Supreme Court, in a case where the plaintiff was a student teacher, ruled that FERPA has its own administrative enforcement scheme that precludes inference of an individual right to sue (*Gonzaga University v. Doe*, 2002).

Conversely, Table 1.1 does not include a federal statute that applies generally, including frequent use in federal civil rights litigation in the education context, but does not provide any independent protection for a substantive interest. Specifically, Section 1983, also known as the Ku Klux Klan Act due to its passage and purpose in the wake of the Civil War, provides for the right to sue the school district and other government officials acting in their official capacity for violations of the Constitution or federal statutes for monetary damages or other judicial remedies. Thus, Section 1983 serves as a handle connecting litigation on behalf of individuals with the various foregoing constitutional provisions and federal statutes that, unlike FERPA, do not have their own supplanting comprehensive enforcement scheme.

Additionally, Table 1.1 does not include two other major federal statutes in the education context—the Individuals with Disabilities Education Act (IDEA) and the No Child Left Behind Act (NCLB). Unlike the statutes in that Table, these two statutes provide substantial, albeit only partial, funding for their respective primary purposes, and they apply only in K–12, not postsecondary, education. They are also distinguishable to the extent that their legislative provisions and their accompanying regulations are unusually extensive and subject to more frequent changes than those in the Table.

Although accompanied by detailed regulations and subject to extensive litigation, the IDEA is entitled to separate treatment, because it applies only to the students that student teachers serve, whereas the "S," i.e., student, entries in Table 1.1 apply to student teachers themselves vis-à-vis their sponsoring institutions of higher education. Although much too complicated for a detailed analysis here, the basic concepts of the IDEA, as explained elsewhere (Zirkel, 2005), include the following:

- eligibility: the student must meet the criteria of one or more of the classifications specified in the IDEA and, by reason thereof, need special education
- free appropriate public education (FAPE): upon meeting the eligibility standards, the student is entitled to special education and related services as documented in an individualized education program (IEP)
- least restrictive environment (LRE): the IEP must be in a placement that provides for interaction with nondisabled students to the maximum extent appropriate
- discipline: for removals of more than 10 days, the IDEA provides for special procedural safeguards, including a manifestation determination, and, in any event, the continuation of FAPE
- dispute resolution: the IDEA provides for two alternate avenues—filing complaints with the state education agency for administrative investigation and filing for impartial due process hearings for administrative adjudication, which is subject to subsequent judicial review
- remedies: beyond prospective orders to correct the IEP or other violation, the most common retrospective remedies for successful adjudications are compensatory education and tuition reimbursement
- parental participation: parents have a special partnership role as members of IEP teams to determine eligibility and FAPE in the LRE and to imple-

ment the dispute resolution provisions for alleged violations of the Act with respect to their child

In contrast, NCLB applies comprehensively, with the unit of accountability collectively being each school and each school district, rather than individually being each child with a disability. Moreover, NCLB is a broad umbrella that includes a variety of formerly separate statutes and a smorgasbord of subjects, including military recruitment, boy scouts, homeless children, persistently dangerous schools, gifted education, student surveys, school-prayer guidelines, and teacher liability protections. The principal component is the former Title I, which focuses on remedial education for economically disadvantaged students. The accountability provisions of NCLB include the following key concepts:

- adequate yearly progress (AYP): state-established and federally approved quantitative standards, including achievement in reading, math, and science during a 12-year period
- disaggregation: applying AYP measures not only to the total student population in the school or district but also to four specified disaggregated groups: students with disabilities, English language learners, poor children, and minority-group students
- sanctions: graduated corrective-action consequences for schools and districts who do not attain AYP, including option to transfer (within the district), "supplemental education services" (i.e., tutoring), and "restructuring"
- personnel standards: special rules for teachers (and paraprofessionals) certified before and after the effective date of the act to achieve the status of being "highly qualified"
- reporting requirements: individual student AYP reports and school/district state report cards to increase parental participation and public information

Illustrating the organic nature of law, NCLB is likely to change significantly in the near future.

Finally, two other federal statutes at least merit mentioning. First is the Children's Internet Protection Act of 2000, which requires schools and libraries that participate in the federal E-rate program to have (1) an Internet safety policy that addresses, for example, cyber bullying, social networking, and hacking, and (2) technology protection measures that block or filter minors' Internet access to specified material, such as pornography. Unlike its two statutory predecessors, this Act withstood a First Amendment challenge at the Supreme Court. The second statute is the Copyright Act of 1976 and its various amendments. These amendments include the Technology, Education, and Copyright Harmonization

Act of 2001, which provides specific guidance as to the application of the fair use doctrine to technological media in the education context. (*United States v. American Library Association, Inc.*).

STATE LAWS: LEADING EXAMPLES

"State law" in this context, as initially shown in Figure 1.2, is a generic phrase that applies not only to various legal sources but also two levels of law. The primary, named level is that of the state in its narrower sense. However, here the other, broader sense is the extension, by way of delegation, to the local level.

Thus, public schools, although typically at the local level, are a delegated decentralization of the state's authority to provide mass education within a specified age range. The various examples of state law that follow are secondarily at the local level. For example, local governments sometimes have documents akin to constitutions in the form of city charters, often have codes or ordinances that are extensions of state legislation, and—via boards of education at the K–12 level or boards of trustees at the postsecondary level—binding policies that are a form of administrative regulations. For the sake of simplicity, the following overview focuses on examples at the state level in the narrow sense but should be understood to apply, by implication, to extend to the broader state/local meaning.

State Constitutions

State constitutions do not often add extra protections to plaintiffs in the public education context, but state statutes and state common law do provide significant additions to the relevant legal building blocks. However, where federal laws provide for the uniformity that cements the foundation of our dual legal system, state laws provide for the variety that allows for customization within the borders of each of the 50 states.

State Legislation and Regulations

Pertinent state laws fit into two categories. First are those that apply more generically but are of interest to student teachers for proper performance of their responsibilities. Consonant with its purpose of providing the foundational building blocks, this chapter provides the leading examples. Second are those state statutes that are specific to student teaching; building on the basic foundation, the next chapter provides an illustrative overview.

This first category consists of various other state statutes and/or their corresponding regulations that are not specific to student teaching but, in their more general coverage, are of direct interest to student teachers. These laws tend to fit into two subcategories in relation to student teachers—those that tend to be common across the 50 states with limited variations and those that exist, again with variation, in only a segment of the states. State statutes in the first, common category that apply directly to student teachers are very few. The leading examples are as follows:

- the increasingly prevalent prerequisite, starting in some states during the practicums preceding student teaching and required in some state laws specifically for student teachers (see Appendix A), for criminal background clearance
- the requirement to report child abuse, when reasonably suspected and with immunity for good faith reporting

Additionally, states commonly have worker's compensation legislation, although these statutes vary as to whether student teachers' are entitled to coverage as employees upon incurring injury during student teaching. Finally, because the most frequent step after successful completion of student teaching is obtaining employment as a public school teacher, the state statutory requirements for teacher certification merit early investigation, including requirements for competency-based testing.

In turn, here are the more frequent examples of the pertinent state statutes in the second, more varying category that apply to cooperating and other teachers and that are purposely stated as questions:

- Does your state law provide for tenure for teachers, and, if so, what are its key provisions?
- Does your state have legislation or regulations for evaluation of teachers, and if so, what are the key provisions?
- Does your state have a law concerning reduction-in-force (RIF) of teaching personnel, and, if so, what are its key provisions?
- Does your state provide for collective bargaining for K–12 teachers, and, if so, what are its key provisions?
- Does your state have a freedom of information act, and, if so, do its provisions apply to your records at the cooperating school?

In addition, the student teacher may benefit from some basic legal literacy in other varying state laws that apply to other key stakeholders beyond the teaching staff, such as students and parents. Examples include state statutes or regulations concerning bullying policies, home schooling, student discipline (e.g., corporal punishment or student suspensions and expulsions), parental neglect, and—as extensions beyond the federal FERPA and PPRA requirements—pupil/parent protection. Note that most of these statutes are specific to the public school context, while the others are much broader in their application.

Tort and Contract Law

The third area of state law consists of tort law and contract law, which are largely a matter of common, i.e., judge-made, law via the doctrine of *stare decisis,* or precedent. To fill the gaps among statutes, judges have developed—in stalagmite fashion—gradually developed clusters of rules on a case-by-case basis, deciding what appears to be a reasonable resolution of new factual circumstances not already covered by codified, i.e., statutory, law.

The doctrine of precedent requires the judge to follow court decisions on the same issue in the same jurisdiction at a higher, appellate level, thus providing for continuity, stability, and predictability. The corresponding latitude for flexibility in institutional learning based on changed values, circumstances, or perspectives is derived from several sources, including (1) the judge's ability—which is reviewable upon appeal—to determine that the issue in the present case is distinguishable, i.e., significantly different, from that of the prior case; (2) the ability of the highest appellate court in the jurisdiction, in an exceptional case, to change its mind and prospectively reverse its prior ruling; and (3) the ability of the judge in one jurisdiction to borrow prior decisions from another jurisdiction that are persuasive, although not binding.

The resulting law of torts, which are civil wrongs not based on contracts, include several categories that, with variations, are common from state to state and that arise in education litigation, whether the institution is public or private. They tend to form a hierarchy according to the extent of fault, with the prevalent remedy being liability for compensatory money damages. Here are the successive categories with examples and defenses from the education context:

- intentional torts:
  e.g., battery, or offensive touching, may arise in the context of corporal punishment or sexual molestation—the defense that may apply in the corporal punishment context is *in loco parentis,* or acting as a reasonable parent would (to the extent allowed by state legislation and local policy)
  e.g., most states recognize various forms of invasion of privacy, such as disclosure of true but private and embarrassing facts – the defenses may be implied consent or a compelling competing interest

e.g., most states have also come to recognize intentional infliction of emotional distress, but they tend to require that the conduct be outrageous to limit abuse of the relative softness of emotional distress, as compared with physical injury
- quasi-intentional torts:
e.g., defamation, consisting in turn of slander, when spoken, and libel, when written—the absolute defenses include that the damaging statement were true or merely opinion, but the most common defense in education is the qualified, or conditional, privilege for good faith criticism that is applicable to the stakeholders, e.g., parents, teachers, administrators, and board members, in the school context
- negligence: i.e., the failure to perform one's legal duty with reasonable diligence directly causing harm to another person, e.g., a student—the defenses are contributory negligence,[4] assumption of risk, and—in the public (but not private) school context—governmental and/or official immunity, which by statute or case law, bars liability on the part of the school district and/or its employees, respectively, in specified circumstances
- strict liability: i.e., liability in limited circumstances without any fault, whether intentional or negligent, typically arising from ultrahazardous activities, such as the use of trampolines—rarely applicable in the school context

As the cases in Chapter III at least partially show, the most common tort in the student teaching context is negligence. In such cases, the student teacher could end up as the plaintiff, the defendant, or a directly related third party, such as a witness. The one subset that is of ethical but not legal concern is instructional negligence, often called "educational malpractice"; the courts have, with very limited exceptions, rejected such claims as contrary to public policy.

The final civil category, which is more a matter of common law than statutory law, is the law of contracts. Although, like constitutional law and tort law, contracts is a whole course in law school, the essential elements of a contract are an offer, an acceptance, and "consideration," meaning in this context something to show that the parties are serious about their agreement. Contrary to the common conception, the general rule is that the contract need not be in writing; however, state statutes often specify limited exceptions, such as employment contracts that have a duration of one year of more.

In the higher education context, for example, the offer is the misnamed letter of acceptance, which is more correctly termed the offer of admission; the acceptance is the student's reply expressing assent; and the consideration is the deposit, which upon submission and receipt shows that both parties have cemented a binding agreement. The terms of the agreement typically include the student handbook, which sets forth the rights and duties of the student and the college or university. Yet, in contrast to employees in K–12 or postsecondary education context, the courts' application of contract theory to higher education students provides extra latitude to the defendant institution based on the traditional doctrine of judicial deference to college/university authorities. For student teaching, the contract with the university would be based upon the catalog, the student teaching handbook, and any other documents that provided a understanding and agreement about the student's and the university's reciprocal responsibilities both procedurally and substantively. Unless the arrangement is one of the unusual special programs whereby the district provides compensation to the student teacher, contract theory would less likely apply to the relationship between the student teacher and the school district than between the student teacher and the sponsoring institution of higher education. Depending on the circumstances, the school district and the university may also have a contractual relationship. However, for the student teacher, interest in contract law may ultimately be stronger in terms of its application—after successful completion of student teaching—to the subsequent hiring and employment process as a teacher.

State Criminal Law

As a final, rather incidental matter, the other form of law is criminal law, which is largely statutory but which may overlap with civil law in cases of intentional torts. For example, a student teacher who engages in sexual or other battery of a student may potentially face four different legal consequences: (1) discipline in the university context, such as dismissal from student teaching; (2) discipline in the school district context, such as cancellation of the student teaching assignment in the district; (3) a tort suit for money damages by the victim's family; and (4) criminal prosecution by the state.

The outcome of each of the foregoing proceedings will not necessarily be the same. As in the famous O. J. Simpson trials, the defendant student teacher could conceivably be found not guilty in the criminal trial in #4 based on the applicable evidentiary standard, which is proof beyond a reasonable doubt, yet be found liable in the civil trial in #3 based on the different and less strict applicable standard of proof, which is preponderance of the evidence. For #1 and #2, the student teacher may file civil suit, raising claims based the foregoing other sources of law, such as breach of contract, statutory discrimination, or—for defendants that are public educational institutions—constitutional violations.

For K-12 students who are minors, criminal prosecution usually means invocation of the state's juvenile justice system. This system varies from state to state but has significant overlap with student discipline and civil litigation for K-12 educational institutions.

LITIGATION TRENDS

At the capstone of the pyramid in Figure 1.2, litigation is where the proverbial tire hits the road, here meaning that the various sources of law intersect with triggering incidents, with the federal and state court being the impartial intermediary to determine the facts and then interpret and apply one of more of the foregoing sources of law to those facts. As summarized elsewhere (Zirkel, 2006c), the trends in education litigation are not what one might surmise from the media or even some promotional education law materials.

First, in terms of frequency, the so-called "explosion" of education litigation ended in the early 1980s; since then, the total volume of K–12 education litigation has been on a gradual downtrend. The leading exceptions are special education and religion-related cases. Second, in terms of outcomes, even during the 1970s and early 1980s, when the courts were more responsive to individual rights, school district defendants won the majority of the cases, and in recent years—led by the Supreme Court (Zirkel, 1998)—the judicial pendulum has swung farther in their favor in the student-initiated cases (D'Angelo and Zirkel, 2008). Higher education litigation has a separate but somewhat similar pattern. For example, the total volume of cases is less than in K–12 education and has continued to increase (Donoso and Zirkel, 2008); yet, the deference to institutional defendants has been pronounced for the entire history of education litigation.

As a result, the overall recommendation is to avoid paralyzing fear about the law generally and liability specifically (Zirkel, 2006b). Rather, a basic legal literacy with regard to student teaching, including knowing what questions to ask and what sources are available for answers, is what is needed and what this volume is designed to provide. The necessary corollaries are (1) to practice preventive law in terms of a selective approach that puts a priority on the identifying and correcting high-risk issues, and at the same time (2) to follow high ethical standards of best, research-based practice and the best interests of children without such confusing "aspirational" professional norms with minimum legal requirements.

Chapter 2

State Statutory Synthesis

This short chapter and the related chart in Appendix A provide an illustrative overview of the state statutes specific to student teaching. It serves as a starting point for ascertaining the applicable policy-type rules for any particular student teaching program. The added pieces should include (1) thorough examination of the cited sections along with any related pertinent statutory provisions; (2) identification and review of any state regulations specific to these statutory provisions; (3) similar effort with regard to the policies and guidelines of responsible state agencies and organizations; and, (4) determination, within the successive layers of such rules, of the applicable policies and standards of the participating institutions, including, for example, any formal agreements between them and official handbooks.

The contents of this chapter provide, in effect, meat to the bones of Appendix A. Thus, both need to be examined in tandem with each other. We provide here a column-by-column and, within each column, row-by-row, highlighting of the state statutory provisions specific to student teaching.

As summarized in Appendix A, several states have statutes specific to student teaching, but they still leave ample latitude for the particular policies of the sponsoring college or university and the cooperating local school district. As the first column of the chart in Appendix A shows, some of the states simply have an enabling act, expressly authorizing school districts and/or institutions of higher education to have student teaching programs. For example, Arkansas provides such authorization for "[a]ny primary or secondary school which has been accredited by the [State] Department of Education" and additionally authorizes (1) the school district to enter into contracts with institutions of higher education, and (2) the state board of education to issue related regulations. As another example, West Virginia's law specifies minimum features of the required inter-institutional agreement, including remuneration for cooperating teachers, adequate facilities, and "participation and instruction with multicultural, at-risk and exceptional children at each programmatic level for which the student teacher seeks certification."

As designated in the second column, some states specify a definition for the requisite terms, such as student teacher or student teaching. For example, three states have a definition for "student teacher," with the alternative term "intern," that is uniform: "a student enrolled in an institution of higher learning approved by the state board of education for teacher training and who is jointly assigned by such institution of higher learning and a board of education to student-teach or intern under the direction of a regularly employed certificated teacher, principal, or other administrator." Instead, Georgia defines "student teaching": "the full-time component of a teacher education program in which a student . . . is jointly assigned by a teacher education institution and a school system, state operated school, or school operated by the United States Department of Defense on a military reservation for classroom experience and which is designated in a teacher education program approved by the [state certification commission for this purpose]."

As displayed in the next column, a few state laws specify either minimum or maximum prerequisites for student teaching. As the minimum side, for example, Michigan requires at least: "(a) high academic achievement; (b) demonstration of successful group work with children as a condition for admission to the teacher preparation curriculum; (c) knowledge of research-based teaching; [and] (d) working knowledge of modern technology and use of computers." On the maximum side, California law limits the prerequisite education courses to nine—or to satisfy the state's English language requirement, twelve—semester units.

The next two columns designate those state laws that specify the authority and protections respectively for student teachers. The "ST Authority" entries that refer to "certified teacher" are of two types. For the more limited type, Mississippi and Nebraska allow the student teacher, under the cooperating teacher's supervision, to perform the responsibilities of a certified teacher. For the more extensive variation, Kentucky and Maryland grant the student teacher, under supervision, the authority of a certified teacher. On the other hand, West Virginia describes the student teacher's authority as that of a substitute teacher.

Conversely, some states provide specific protections for student teachers, with Kentucky being the only one to accompany the responsibilities of certified teachers with their corresponding protections. The other state laws in this category do so expressly only on this protection side. For example, Arkansas grants student teachers the same "immunities" as teachers have, whereas North Carolina provides student teachers, while performing their assigned teaching, with the "protections" that certified teachers have. The statutes in both Iowa and New Jersey specifically provide save-harmless and indemnification protections that apply in those states to school officers and employees.

The penultimate column illustrates the varying statutory specifications for the cooperating teacher. For example, Nebraska specifies a legal duty for the cooperating teacher: "in cooperation with the principal and the representative of the teacher-preparation institution, to assign to the student teacher responsibilities and duties that will provide adequate preparation for teaching." As a much more unusual example, Georgia law provides for special certification in "supervising teacher services."

Moreover, Iowa legislation has more than one statutory provision for cooperating teachers: (1) establishment of a cooperating teacher incentive program that requires the institution of higher education to provide, with specified variations, "either a monetary recompense or a reduction in tuition for graduate hours of coursework equivalent to the value of the monetary recompense"; and (2) requirement for the sponsoring higher education institutions to provide an annual workshop for cooperating teachers that "shall define the objectives of the student teaching experience, review the responsibilities of the cooperating teacher, and provide the cooperating teacher other information and assistance the institution deems necessary." One other state law addresses compensation along with qualifications; more specifically, Pennsylvania legislation requires the state colleges to have a salary schedule, starting with a minimum of $75 per student teacher, for each cooperating teacher, who must have a baccalaureate degree and at least three years public school teaching experience.

The final column displays the miscellaneous additional pertinent provisions. For example, California expressly permits what appears to be a special variation of the more general student teaching option—a district intern program that has various specified features, including the selection of cooperating teacher (1) who must "possess valid certification at the same level, or of the same type of credential, as the district interns they serve," and (2) who is selected via "a competitive process adopted by the [school] board after consultation with the exclusive teacher representative unit [i.e., the union] or by personnel employed by institutions of higher education to supervise student teachers."

As a more limited unusual variation, Georgia encourages the relevant state agencies to facilitate "assigning student teachers to as many classes within each school system's Summer Opportunity Program as possible."[1] Similarly, in its legislation that authorizes specified uses of non-certificated personnel, Illinois provides a caveat that within certain specified conditions "[n]othing in this Section shall require constant supervision of a student teacher enrolled in a student teaching course at a college or university."

Notably, in addition to its other relatively detailed statutory provisions, Iowa specifies both minimum time periods—12 weeks for student teaching along with at least 50 hours of field experiences, including 10 hours before acceptance into the teacher education program—and minimum experiences, including "a mock evaluation performed by the cooperating teacher . . . [that] shall not be used as an assessment tool by the practitioner preparation program." At the same time, Iowa requires institutions of higher education to have specific forms and procedures for the evaluation of student teachers that evidence "a cooperative process that involves both the faculty member supervising the student teacher and the cooperating teacher."

Unusually, Kansas authorizes the state board of education to issue "student teaching licenses" along with related regulations. Similarly notable, Maryland provides student teachers with employee status for the limited purpose of liability insurance and workers' compensation coverage. Michigan has an unusual provision specific to charter schools, which its statutes refer to as "public school academies":

> If a district or an employee of a district discriminates against a [student teacher] in the district because the [sponsoring] state university . . . serves as the authorizing body for 1 or more public school academies, the district forfeits an amount equal to 10% of [its state funding].

The other remarkable variations are (1) Nevada's statutory authorization, with specific conditions, for student teachers to serve as substitute teachers; (2) South Carolina's statutory requirement for each sponsoring institution of higher education to provide specified evaluation and assistance requirements, including "assistance, training, and counseling to the student teacher to overcome any identified deficiencies"; (3) Washington state's legislation provision, with a specified mission, that "the professional educator standards board, from appropriated funds, shall establish a network of student teaching centers"; and (4) West Virginia's specific allowance for student teaching in nonpublic schools as an alternative to public school placements.

In sum, less than half the states have statutes specific to student teaching, and only a handful—e.g., Iowa, Kentucky, Maryland, Michigan and North Carolina—appear to provide more than one or two pertinent provisions. The terminology varies, such as the use of "intern" for student teacher and "supervising teacher" for what we generically refer to as cooperating teacher, but the basic definitions, where provided, are similar. The state legislatures have largely left the selection and roles of student teachers to other levels of state and local determination, with a few states providing the protections—largely in terms of litigation benefits, such as immunity or indemnification—of regular teachers. Likely due to the political clout of teacher organizations, the states tend to have legislated more provisions specifically for the cooperating teacher than the student teacher, with the variations in such provisions—for example, Georgia's certification for supervising teachers—being rather remarkable. Even more noteworthy is the variety of miscellaneous other provisions, such as Maryland's license and insurance-type benefits for student teachers.

Thus, typical of the United States' legal framework, the states serve as laboratories for testing innovative ideas, with cross-fertilization and customization among state statutes and delegated discretion to other levels of policymaking. This heretofore unexplored area of student teaching law warrants further data collection, analysis, and assessment.

Chapter 3

Case Law Synthesis

Student teachers, being apprentices and in a hybrid transitional role between students and employees, would appear to be prime sources of education litigation. Moreover, student teaching, being a rather specialized and special professional experience, presents the rather distinctive formulation or application of legal issues. Nevertheless, the professional literature is lacking in terms of comprehensive and current information about litigation concerning student teachers and student teaching.

More specifically, only two studies came close to identifying the pertinent court cases, but they are incomplete and out-of-date. In the first of these studies, Swalls (1976) found 14 published court cases between 1906 and 1975 that he divided into four categories: a) legal authority to permit student teaching in public schools ($n = 5$); b) legal authority for the acceptance, assignment, and dismissal of student teachers ($n = 4$); c) certification and welfare of student teachers ($n = 3$); and d) tort liability of student teachers ($n = 2$). His description of each case was cursory, and the boundaries of his study were not well defined.

In the second study, which was a dissertation, Hall (1989) reviewed state statutes, case law, and attorney general opinions to analyze the legal status of student teachers in relationship to higher education institutions and to the public schools. Within this limited scope, Hall identified 26 published court decisions that she divided into two sections based on the party being sued, i.e., higher education institution or local cooperating school. She further classified the 11 cases where the sponsoring college or university was a defendant and the 15 cases where the cooperating school district was a defendant, but the coverage was neither comprehensive nor complete, and the classifications did not have a consistent basis. Moreover, although finding a doubling of the cases in two decades, her results are obviously dated and did not include corresponding analysis of the outcomes of the cases.

As a result, this chapter provides a comprehensive synthesis of published case law concerning student teaching. We thoroughly searched both of the major legal databases—LEXIS and Westlaw[1]—to find court decisions where student teachers were either the plaintiffs or defendants, or where student teaching was at issue even if the student teacher was only a third party. We included variant search terms, such as "intern" and "practicum," ultimately selecting cases based on whether the role or experience fit the general meaning of student teacher or student teaching.

The boundary is not a bright line, requiring discretionary judgment at the margins. For example, we excluded as too peripheral a First Amendment retaliation case where one of the various alleged reasons for the firing of the plaintiff-teacher was his statement in support of his former student teacher (*Whitsel v. Southeast Local School District*, 1973) and another more recent such case where one of the various alleged reasons for not hiring the plaintiff-teacher was what he said to and about a student teacher (*Watson v. Connelly*, 2008). Another marginal exclusion was a highly publicized student peer harassment case where the graphic sexual conduct occurred in a classroom that school officials had left to the supervision of a student teacher (*D.R. v. Middle Bucks Area Vocational Technical School*, 1992). Similarly, a student's challenge to a failing grade in a required education course prior to student teaching did not seem quite close enough for inclusion (*Head v. Board of Trustees of California State University*, 2007). Conversely, there were other close calls where we gave the benefit of the doubt in favor of inclusion—for example, a case where student teachers were part of a larger group of dismissed students (*Scott v. Alabama State Board of Education*, 1969) and another where the student was in an "advanced practicum" as part of a graduate teacher certification program (*Nickerson v. University of Alaska*, 1999).

The final result of this search and selection process consisted of 47 cases (see Appendix B). For the purpose of this chapter, we divided them into the four successive phases of student teaching: (1) admission/placement of student teachers, (2) conditions of student teaching, (3) dismissal of student teachers, and (4) taxation issues for student teaching. In each of these four successive sections, we present the court decisions in chronological order within operational subcategories (e.g., basis for non-placement), rather than legal subcategories (e.g., nature of litigation claim).

ADMISSION/PLACEMENT OF STUDENT TEACHERS

The first of the four categories includes court cases where students challenged institutional decisions that prevented them from starting their student teaching. We divided these court decisions into two subcategories based on the reason for their non-placement: (1) formal prerequisites for student teaching (four cases), and (2) other pertinent conduct (three cases). In the four court cases in the first subcategory, higher institutions did not allow the students to start student teaching due to their academic deficiencies. In the four court cases in the second category, the higher education institutions either refused to find placement or could not find placement for students due to behavior unrelated to their academic performance or teaching skills. Overall, the cases in both subcategories reveal the wide variety of the plaintiff-students' claims and the general tendency in favor of the defendant institutions.

Formal Prerequisites

In the earliest court case in this subcategory, the federal Ninth Circuit Court of Appeals affirmed the federal trial court's summary denial of a former student's claim that one of the California state universities violated his First Amendment freedom of expression in not allowing him to start his student teaching assignment (*Holt v. Munitz,* 1996). Assuming without deciding that his participation in a press conference in response to a controversial racial incident—the police beating of Rodney King—was protected expression, the court pointed to undisputed evidence that the reason for his removal was his failure to complete a final examination that was a prerequisite to partake in student teaching. Thus, the university proved that it would have disallowed him from participating in student teaching regardless of any protected expression, defeating his claim.

However, probably because Holt proceeded in court *pro se*, i.e., without a lawyer, the court did not address the potential counter-argument that the freedom of expression framework for students, rather than that for public employees, should have applied, particularly at this incipient stage of student teaching.

In a more recent case, a private college denied Angeline Furlong entrance into student teaching on the basis of her written communication skills (*Furlong v. Carroll College,* 2001). The college had accepted her into the teacher education program only conditionally because of the poor initial essay; and, given a second opportunity, the subsequent essay that she submitted with her application was deemed deficient as well. The condition was that she would pursue a course of independent study to address and remedy her deficiencies in her writing skills. According to the college officials, Furlong abandoned the program prior to student teaching, and, in any event, did not show the requisite improvement in basic grammatical skills for placement. According to Furlong, who filed suit in state court, the college officials breached the duty to prepare her for the profession of teaching, thus constituting negligence or breach of contract.

The Montana trial court granted the college's motion for summary judgment against Furlong. First, the court examined the precedents and concluded that Montana does not recognize a claim against a college or its agents for inadequate education, whether called negligence or educational malpractice. Second, the court rejected her claim of implied contractual obligations on the college's part, concluding that (1) the college catalog stated the requirements for admission into the teacher education major, including the student's submission and faculty's assessment of a written essay and the option of conditional admissions; (2) the college's representatives indisputably had followed these express contractual requirements; and (3) an express contract supersedes any implied contract on the same subject matter. Furlong did not appeal this trial court decision.

Soon thereafter, Alaska's highest court affirmed the trial court's dismissal of another *pro se* claim, along with its order for the plaintiff student to pay $3,000 to the defendant university in attorneys' fees (*Hunt v. University of Alaska,* 2002). In this case, the university's school of education granted contingent admission to the application of a third-year student with a 3.58 GPA. The contingency, based on his relatively low grades—although none below a "C"—in English and the rather blatant deficiencies in his application essays, was that he pass the reading and writing part of the Praxis exam. After starting the program, Hunt failed both required parts. He continued in the methods courses, based on a partial waiver, but again failed the required parts the following semester. When the faculty refused to allow him to take student teaching, the student had a hearing before the university's academic appeals committee, which upheld the elementary education faculty's decision.

Hunt's *pro se* lawsuit suffered the same fate as the preceding cases. First, his Fourteenth Amendment equal protection claim failed because he failed to prove that the program had allowed other students with contingent admissions to take the student teaching course without first fulfilling their contingency. Second, his breach of contract claim did not succeed based on the judicial tradition of deference to the academic discretion of university faculty members and committees. Third, his resort to state statutes and university policies against misleading information went for naught because the court deemed the Praxis requirement to be reasonable. Finally, the court concluded that state law allowed for the attorneys' fees award and that the plaintiff focused on the wrong rule of civil procedure.

Undaunted, Hunt filed a motion for a new trial based on newly discovered evidence. The trial court denied his motion. On appeal, Alaska's highest court affirmed, concluding that this evidence "even when viewed in the most favorable light, reveals only that the [university] allowed other students like Hunt to proceed to the methods courses before passing the exam . . . [but] not suggest that the students were allowed to proceed to student teaching" (p. *7).[2] The court also upheld the lower court's order for Hunt to pay the university $3,000, which represented 30% of its attorney's fees.

In the latest court decision in this subcategory (*Thomas v. Hamline University*, 2008), the student, Jenelle Thomas, transferred to the defendant-university to pursue majors in both music and education as part of the music education licensure program. When she started experiencing problems in her classes, her academic advisor held a meeting with the student, who in turn informed the advisor that she suffered from depression. Her professors provided accommodations for her needs; however, the student continued to experience problems and exhibit a negative attitude. As a result, her academic advisor sent an e-mail to the department chair expressing the belief that the student was not suitable to be a school teacher. Offering the student one final opportunity, the academic advisor and other faculty suggested that she teach a lesson they could observe, but the student declined. The university disallowed her to pursue licensure in music education due to her failure both to attain an acceptable grade point average in her education courses and to fulfill the observation requirement.

Thomas sued the university on the basis of disability discrimination and the academic advisor for allegedly aiding and abetting the college in discriminating against her. She sought relief under the ADA and the parallel provisions of the Minnesota Human Rights Act (MHRA). Because the university filed a motion for summary judgment, the federal district court assumed as true the allegations that the student had a disability. Similarly, the university did not dispute its coverage under Title III of the ADA, which applies to private entities that own or operate a place of public accommodation, as well as the MHRA. Thus, the issue was whether the university engaged in disparate treatment of Thomas based on her disability by requiring her to agree to a teaching observation as a precondition for participating in student teaching and, thus, for continuing to pursue licensure.

The court determined that the academic advisor's professional judgment was strong evidence the university had good reason to be concerned about

Thomas's ability to satisfy state certification standards that require teachers " . . . to create a positive learning environment and expect teachers to collaborate with colleagues, seek and give feedback with both colleagues and students, and establish a positive climate in both the classroom and in the school as a whole" (p. *4). The academic advisor had identified characteristics of the student's personality and demeanor that conflicted with the skill set of a successful teacher and had attempted to address that behavior through an observation, an intervention that the university had employed when it had similar concerns with other students' ability to perform. Thus, the court concluded that there was no evidence to suggest that her disability was the motivating factor for the college's decision to require an observation. The aiding and abetting charge also failed due to the rejection of the first claim.

Other Pertinent Conduct

In the earliest decision in this subcategory—*Robinson v. University of Miami* (1958)—a private university "withdrew its acceptance" (p. 443) after the principal of the cooperating school called the university's attention to a letter that the student had written on atheism in a local newspaper. After meeting with the student, the university's committee on student teaching determined that he was not only fanatical in his views in favor of atheism but also would seek to impose them on students he might teach. The student sued, claiming that the university violated the contract of enrollment it had with him.

The appellate court concluded the University of Miami had not acted arbitrarily or with malice and that it had a right to withdraw a student at any time after his acceptance without necessity of furnishing him with a reason or cause. Additionally, the court reasoned that the university has an "obligation" not to graduate and thereby place "the stamp of its academic approval" on a new teacher "having fanatical ideas" (p. 444) on atheism.

More than a decade later, in *James v. West Virginia Board of Regents* (1971), the defendant public college failed to place an African-American student teacher in a public school of his choice after the college had suspended him from his original student teaching location, which was a local high school. The suspension had arisen in the wake of the bombing of the college's physical education building. The police arrested him, along with several other students who had participated in racial demonstrations, charging them with felonious conspiracy to bomb said building, and the resulting media coverage branded him as a militant. Following the dismissal of the charges, the student teacher requested readmission to the college and a student teaching assignment in one of public schools in the immediate county.

Due to James' reputation, the college was unable to arrange a placement of his choice but succeeded in assigning him to a school in another county. Refusing the assignment, James sued the state board of regents, college officials, and the local county school board in federal court, claiming violations of the First Amendment's expression and assembly clauses and the Fourteenth Amendment's due process and equal protection clauses.

First, the federal district court in West Virginia summarily rejected James' constitutional claims against the college defendants, concluding that they had fulfilled their "duty of making a good faith effort to place those of its students majoring in education in an accredited school [for student teaching]" despite "much provocation from him" (p. 227). Specific to the First Amendment, the court concluded that his threatening conduct went beyond the protection of the speech and assembly clauses.

Second, the court similarly denied James' constitutional claims against the school district. Specific to Fourteenth Amendment substantive due process and equal protection, the court concluded that the refusal of the school officials to accept the student teacher was solely predicated on his reputation as a militant on and off campus, which was reasonable and not racial. The court reasoned that character is a "relevant . . . and proper" (p. 228) selection criterion for student teachers and that James had received the same treatment as white applicants. The Fourth Circuit Court of Appeals subsequently summarily affirmed the district court's decision.

Later the same year, the federal district court in North Carolina summarily rejected another student teacher's constitutional claim (*Lai v. Board of Trustees of East Carolina University,* 1971). Previously, the police in another state had arrested the student, charging him with drug possession; however, the prosecution dropped the charges. Then, the student submitted a student teaching application that the director rejected. Subsequently, at the direction of the university's president, the education committee provided the student with notice and a hearing wherein he admitted that he had smoked marijuana, resulting in the committee affirming the director's decision. The student filed suit against the university, claiming that the defendants' actions a) were arbitrary and capricious, b) constituted cruel and unusual punishment, c) constituted double jeopardy, and d) denied him due process of law.

In a brief, one-page opinion, the federal district court dismissed Lai's claims. Specifically addressing only his procedural due process and his arbitrary and capricious claims, the court concluded that the university's hearing process met the fundamental fairness standard and that "absent a showing that university authorities acted in bad faith or exercised their discretion arbitrarily, [the university officials] are entitled to wide discretion in the regulation of the training of their students" (p. 906).

CONDITIONS OF STUDENT TEACHING

The second category consists of 14 court cases, which we further divided into four subcategories: (1) injuries to student teachers, which consists of four cases; (2) injuries to students, representing three cases; (3) accommodations for student teachers with disabilities, which was a single court decision; and (4) legality of student teaching arrangement, consisting of six cases. Overall, these court decisions shed light on the historical development of student teaching to what it has become today, which the last subcategory clearly illustrates. They also reveal the wide and evolving range of issues that can arise during student teaching, from traditional state common law claims based on injuries to student teachers or the students under their care to federal discrimination claims based on the relatively recent legislative protection for individuals—including student teachers—with disabilities.

Injuries to Student Teachers

In the earliest case in this subcategory, the employment status of a student teacher arose in the context of state worker's compensation legislation. More specifically, in *Betts v. Ann Arbor Public Schools* (1978), a student teacher incurred a serious eye injury at his school district placement and filed a claim for worker's compensation benefits. The applicable state agency granted the claim, and the school district sought judicial review. The lower court ruled in favor of the school district, reasoning that he was not an employee. However, upon the student-teacher's appeal, Michigan's highest court reinstated his benefits, concluding that "public employee" under the state's worker's disability compensation statute had a broader definition of "employee" in the private sector. This broader scope extended to student teachers because, although they did not receive money, they were not volunteers; instead, the district chose to accept their beneficial services, and in return the student teachers received training, college credit toward graduation, and fulfillment of the prerequisites for a provisional teaching certificate.

Several years later, an appellate court denied a student teacher's claim of her university's liability for negligence (*Dello v. State,* 1984). More specifically, the student teacher fell and was injured on a slippery, snow-filled path upon exiting the rear of the university's campus elementary school building at the end of the school day. She claimed that the school's failure to shovel, salt, and sand the path amounted to negligence. The trial court summarily rejected her claim, and the appellate court affirmed the dismissal. The reasons were that (1) the path went through the school's fenced-in and gated playground area, causing the university's grounds supervisor to conclude that shoveling or plowing the path would cause mounds that posed an attractive nuisance and hazardous condition for the children, and (2) the student teacher assumed the risk because she had traveled on the path earlier in the day and was able to further perceive the danger due to the large glass panel in the rear exit door.

In another common law case one year later, the student teacher was again the plaintiff, but the defendant was a private company (*Arbegast v. Board of Education*, 1985). In this New York case, the student teacher, Christy Arbegast, incurred permanent injury to her arm when she participated in a fund-raising event—a donkey basketball game—for the senior class. She originally sued the school board and the private company that provided the animals and equipment, which included helmets for the participants, but she settled her claim with the board prior to the trial.

Arbegast's two alternate claims against the company were strict liability and negligence, both based on the donkeys' vicious propensities. The company's defense was express assumption of the risk, specifically based on its employee's warnings to the participants that donkeys buck and put their heads down, causing people to fall off, and that participation was at their own risk. The jury decided in favor of the defendant-company, finding that although the assigned donkey had injury-producing tendencies and that the company had known about them, its employee had made the plaintiff-student teacher aware of the risk, and she had voluntarily agreed to participate. On appeal, the New York's highest court upheld the judgment in the company's favor, concluding that the state's particular statute, which established a proportional form of contributory negligence called purely comparative negligence, did not affect the jury's conclusion that Arbegast had assumed the risk in this case.

The outcome of the Arbegast case should not be overgeneralized. Both negligence and strict liability cases will depend not only on the particular facts, but also the specifics of these two torts and their defenses under state law. As Chapter I points out, tort law represents a common theme with considerable variations from state to state. Moreover, the particular contours of the law in a given state may change over time via court decisions or state statutes.

In the most recent case in this subcategory, a student teacher, who was doing her 12-credit internship in an elementary school special education class, sustained injury when one of the students shoved her from behind into a wall (*Orange County School Board v. Powers*, 2007). She completed an incident report, per school district policy, but when she inquired about medical treatment, the district's representative advised her to contact the sponsoring university. She did so, but the university officials informed her that their insurance policy did not cover injuries incurred in student teaching. She then filed for benefits from the school district's workers' compensation plan. Despite the district's assertions to the contrary, the workers' compensation judge in Florida ruled that Powers was a district employee and, thus, entitled to benefits. The district filed an appeal.

The appellate court reversed the decision that had been in the student teacher's favor. The appeals court concluded that Powers did not meet the definition of employee in Florida's workers' compensation statute, which required "remuneration." The appellate court's reasoning was that the benefit she had received in exchange for tuition did not fit within the meaning of this term.

Powers' two alternative arguments fell short of the mark. She cited a Florida statute that provided student teachers with the same rights accorded to certified teachers, with the exception of collective bargaining. In response, the appeals court concluded that in the absence of a provision in this statute superseding the workers' compensation law, her failure to qualify under that law's definition of employee was fatal to her claim. Similarly, she pointed to a statute that provided workers' compensation benefits to "volunteer workers." In response, the appellate court reiterated that she was student teaching for her own purpose, which was to complete certification requirements, not to aid the school, thereby not fitting within this alternate eligibility category.

Injuries to Students

In an early negligence case (*Gardner v. State*, 1939), New York's highest court upheld the judgment in favor of a seventh grade girl who sustained injuries in the course of performing a head stand during a physical education class in a state college's lab school. One teacher was in charge, and the students were in small groups throughout the gym and the gym foyer, each under the supervision of a student teacher. The parents of the injured student claimed that the school had failed not only to give their daughter proper preparatory strengthening exercises but also to provide her with a qualified teacher to supervise the instruction.

In cryptically concluding, without further explanation, that the "failure to instruct the [child] pursuant to the customary method was the proximate cause of her injuries" (p. 212), the appellate court was arguably referring to the work of regular, not the student, teacher. In any event, the Gardners did not sue the student teacher; instead, the defendant was the governmental entity that operated the school, because its budget obviously represented the "deeper pocket" for money damages. Moreover, the dissenting judge would have reversed on the basis of the student's contributory negligence.

Exactly four decades later, the Nebraska Supreme Court upheld a judgment for approximately $54,000 against a school district in a negligence case (*Brahatcek v. Millard School District,* 1979). During golf instruction in the district's physical education (PE) program, one ninth grader had accidentally killed another one on the follow through of his golf swing. One teacher was in charge of two combined classes that day; her counterpart, the boys' PE teacher, was absent, and the student teacher had taken his place.

In affirming the trial court's verdict in favor of the Brahatceks, one of the appellate court's key conclusions was that "there was ineffective observation and attention on the part of the student teacher when ordinary care or supervision would have prevented the occurrence which resulted in the death" (p. 687). Here again, the family of the deceased student sued the district, not the student teacher, presumably because the student teacher's negligence could be attributed to the district, either via the *respondeat superior* doctrine or due to the teacher in charge or the principal not having sufficiently supervised the student teacher.

Most recently, a Connecticut trial court issued an "unpublished" opinion, meaning here in its narrow sense one that is not official precedent, in response to another negligence suit coincidentally arising from a student's inadvertent swing of a golf club (*Brown v. Acorn Acres, Inc.,* 2000). In this case, the resulting injury was to a seventh grader during a field trip to a miniature golf course, and the court's opinion was in the form of two preliminary rulings. Only one of the two rulings related at all to the student teacher, who had worked with five regular teachers to supervise the field trip.

More specifically, one of the parents' claims in *Brown* was that this group of six chaperones was negligent in their supervision of the students. The parents brought this claim under a Connecticut statute that obligated school boards to indemnify employees who are liable for damages. In dismissing this claim, the court concluded that the purpose of this statute was to provide employees with protection, not to provide third parties with a right to sue. In arriving at this general conclusion, the court did not specifically and separately address whether the student teacher was an employee covered under the umbrella of the indemnification statute. In any event, the plaintiff-parents targeted the deeper pockets of the school district and the owner of the miniature golf course, not naming the student teacher or the five regular staff members as defendants.

Accommodations for Student Teachers with Disabilities

A federal appellate court upheld the rejection, based on untimeliness, of a former student teacher's claim of disability discrimination under § 504 and the ADA (*Everett v. Cobb County School District,* 1998). The plaintiff had multiple sclerosis and bilateral joint dysfunction, which required her reliance on an electrically-powered scooter for mobility. She alleged that during student teaching the supervising teacher had refused to allow her to use the scooter in the classroom and had made various disparaging comments about her disability. Although the supervising teacher recommended a grade of "Unsatisfactory," the college faculty decided to give student teacher Everett an "Incomplete." Everett was obviously not satisfied; she sued both the college and the school district under these two interrelated federal disability discrimination statutes.

However, the fatal problem with Everett's suit was that she did not file it on time. The Eleventh Circuit Court of Appeals affirmed the federal district court's conclusion that the applicable limitations period was two years, commencing when Everett first received notification of the Incomplete. She filed suit exactly two years after receiving the letter confirming the faculty's decision, but that letter was one week after she received the grade. Applying the timeline strictly, the appellate court upheld the dismissal of her claim.

Legality of Student Teaching Arrangement

In the six cases in this subcategory, the legality of either student teaching generally or the student teacher role specifically was at issue, and the basis of the court's decision in five of the cases was a state statute. In an early cluster of cases, the issue was whether school districts that participated in student teaching programs were in violation of their respective state enabling statutes.

In the first and oldest case, student teachers were innocent bystanders but, just as obviously, interested third parties. More specifically, in *Lindblad v. Board of Education* (1906), pursuant to contract, a state university used up to nine grades of public schools in the nearby school district as practice schools. In each grade, a staff member, known as a critic teacher, supervised students from the university, who taught subjects to the pupils of the schools. By the act incorporating the town in which the student teaching took place, the town managed and controlled the common schools. Arguing that the town could not delegate those powers, a taxpayer sued, seeking to enjoin the town's board of education from continuing this practice.

The state trial court denied the motion, and the appellate court affirmed. However, upon review, the Supreme Court of Illinois ruled that under the pertinent legislation the local school board was without authority to employ teachers to perform the duties of the critic teachers. Thus, the contract by which the board employed each of the critic teachers was illegal and void, and the payment of those teachers out of the funds of the public school was an unlawful diversion of public money. Such an unlawful contract was an injury to the taxpayer, and the state's highest court reversed the denial of the taxpayer's motion to enjoin the board of education from employing critic teachers. The court commented that the resulting problem was within the authority of the state legislature, not the court, to address.

By way of partial contrast, approximately a decade later West Virginia's highest court concluded that a local school district's operation of a model school for the "practice work" of student teachers under the supervision of "critic teachers" was within the discretion of the local board under the state statute authorizing local board to establish and maintain public schools (*Spedden v. Board of Education*, 1914). Here, the specific focus was the student teacher, not the critic teacher. Interpreting said statute, the court reasoned as follows:

> The law requires the employment of competent teachers, but there is no express exclusion of assistant or under teachers. The student teachers are not employed . . . [T]he regularly employed, competent teachers stand over them . . . This involves no delegation of their powers. It is a mere departure or variation in methods, which, in the opinion of some people, is unwise and inefficient, and, in the opinion of others, efficient and helpful . . . [Such] questions [are] . . . matters for determination by the board, not the courts nor the citizens (pp. 726–727).

Again showing the limited role of the courts in such state statutory matters, a California appellate court upheld the county board of education's charge of a fee, then $2, for a state-required certificate for student teaching (*Blanchard v. Keppel*, 1916). Declining to review the reasonableness of the policy, the court concluded: "The language of the Code being in this instance clear and unmistakable, we cannot indulge in a discussion about what the Legislature ought to have intended to do" (p. 691).

Also shortly after the West Virginia case but much closer as to its issue than the California case, Iowa's highest court upheld a district's arrangement with a local teacher's college that provided a model school for student teachers where the cooperating teacher received part of their pay from the teachers college (*Clay v. Independent School District*, 1919). A group of taxpayers sued, seeking to discontinue the work of the student teachers and the partial payments by the college. In response, the school district arranged with the state education department to issue provisional teaching certificates to the student teachers, as then allowed under state law.

The state's supreme court viewed this solution as removing the basis for Clay's and the other taxpayers' suit, but the following dicta indirectly supported the student teachers even without that solution: "It is very doubtful . . . whether the statute prohibiting the employment of uncertified teachers has any application to a case where the person in question does no more than render gratuitous temporary incidental assistance to a competent and duly certified teacher, who has the room and pupils in her immediate charge and control" (p. 51). As in the California case, the appeals court viewed the matter as discretionary for the school district, explaining: "We do not hold, and it is not within our province to say, that in adopting this plan of co-operation with the college the board did that which was wisest or best, though if that were a decisive consideration it would not be difficult to advance many plausible arguments in its favor" (p. 52).

Almost six and a half decades later, the role of student teacher was at issue within the general context of a state statute mandating teacher-board collective bargaining and within the specific context of membership in the unit represented by the teachers union (*Arrowhead United Teachers Organization v. Wisconsin Employment Relations Commission,* 1984). In this case, the Wisconsin agency that administers the collective bargaining statute for public employees had determined that the particular student teachers at issue did not have a sufficient "community of interest" with the full-time and regular part-time professional employees represented by the union.

More specifically, these student teachers were interns in a special University of Wisconsin program. This program internship was an alternate way to fulfill the student teaching requirement for state certification; unlike the traditional route, the program interns were district employees for one semester, receiving a stipend of $2,000 and a benefit of five days' sick leave during this temporary employment. They had "intern teaching licenses" and similar responsibilities to those of regular teachers, except that they had fewer classes to teach and more study halls and prep periods.

Nevertheless, the Supreme Court of Wisconsin upheld the agency's unit determination, concluding that "the interns remain primarily students" and that "academic interests are alien to the usual employment relationship, which centers around economic interests . . . [and which is] concerned mainly with career-length objectives such as benefits, wages, retirement, etc." (p. 718).

In the last case in this subcategory, the basis was the federal constitution, specifically the First Amendment's establishment clause, rather than state statutory law (*Stark v. St. Cloud State University,* 1985). In this case, at the request of two parochial schools a public university had a policy allowing teacher education students to satisfy their student teaching requirements at parochial schools, and two or three individuals had done so. A pair of plaintiffs—a taxpayer and a member of the student teaching faculty—sued in federal court, alleging that the policy violated the First Amendment's establishment clause. The Eighth Circuit Court of Appeals upheld the district court's decision against the state university, concluding that the policy had a secular purpose but that its primary effect communicated a message of government endorsement of pervasively sectarian parochial schools.

Due to the fluidity of the Supreme Court's establishment clause jurisprudence, which includes both overruling of some of the precedents on which the Eighth Circuit relied and confirmation of the endorsement criterion, it is unclear whether the outcome of this decision is generalizable today.

DISMISSAL OF STUDENT TEACHERS

The dismissal category accounts for more cases than any other category—22 court decisions. These cases reflect, in the rearview mirror, the many facets of student teaching. The requisites and responsibilities of a student teacher are akin to those of full-time teachers, including content knowledge, its effective delivery, classroom management, moral conduct, and appropriate communication with students, colleagues, and superiors. Similar to their regular teacher counterparts, compliance with institutional policies and familiarity with education law can also be a factor in the student teacher's continuance or dismissal. Yet, the difficulties for student teachers are even more obvious due to their apprentice-like inexperience and their dual status as students and teachers.

Continuing our comparison of student teachers to full-fledged teachers, we borrowed from the framework of teacher tenure laws to organize the court decisions in this predominant category. Those states that have teacher tenure laws restrict the reasons for termination to just cause or, more often, specific grounds that they recognize as just cause. The most common grounds, although varying in terminology, tend to be incompetence, immorality, and insubordination. Other variations include intemperance and incapacity. These grounds are obviously broad and often overlapping. The student teacher dismissal cases tended to fit into four subcategories depending on the cause, or grounds: (1) immorality—three cases, (2) insubordination or intemperance—six cases, (3) incompetence—six cases, and (4) wrongful evaluation—seven cases. As with the other categories, these divisions and placement within them are only approximate, particularly because—in the absence of the tenure framework—the sponsoring university and cooperating school district were not required to specify these particular grounds.

Immorality

Immorality has a variable meaning that in some jurisdictions requires a nexus to classroom performance. Here, we used the broad meaning, without the nexus requirement, and included not only conduct generally associated with sexual immorality or crimes but also conduct that violated community mores, such as dishonesty, lying, or fraud.

In the earliest case in this subcategory, the constitutional claims of an individual student teacher summarily ended in defeat (*Rowe v. Chandler,* 1971). The principal of the high school had summoned Rowe to his office and summarily discontinued his student teaching at the school based on numerous rumors that he had engaged in immoral and unprofessional conduct toward students. As a result, the college, a private institution, dropped the student teacher from its certification program. Seeking monetary damages and other relief, the student teacher sued, claiming that the college and the school officials had conspired together under color of state law to deprive him of due process and equal protection of law.

First, the court dismissed Rowe's governmental conspiracy claim because the defendant college was a private institution and its cooperative relationship with the public school was insufficient to establish "the requisite state action" (p. 340). Second, for the same basic reason, the court dismissed the college from Rowe's procedural due process claim. Third, his procedural due process claim against the public school official failed because, although the principal represented a governmental entity, Rowe lacked a property right, i.e., legitimate entitlement or reasonable expectation, to perform his student teaching at that particular public school; the plaintiff student teacher "had no contractual relationship with [the school] justifying a student teaching tenure" (p. 341) and had no other basis under state law for the requisite entitlement or expectation.

Interestingly, in dicta, the *Rowe* court acknowledged that the principal was criticizable for "an absolute lack of a hearing procedure" (p. 341) and that he "had a duty of decency to see that he was not acting upon false accusation" (p. 341); yet, the court further commented, "[the principal's] duty to protect the students, their parents, and the school board from potentially abrasive and unpleasant events was a transcendent one, fully justifying his action" (p. 341).

The next case arose three decades later, and its fit in this subcategory is marginal, because the triggering action was the refusal to provide the requisite recommendation after, rather than the actual dismissal during, student teaching. Nevertheless, we gave the benefit of the doubt in favor of inclusion because it is a published precedent, even reaching the U.S. Supreme Court on one of the student teacher's claims (*Doe v. Gonzaga University*, 2001/2002). The case started with two staff members' response to allegations that John Doe, a student in the teacher education program at a private university, allegedly committed date rape on a female student. The alleged victim had not filed a formal complaint with the university. However, based on statements by a friend, which the alleged victim later denied, and by two faculty members, which she also largely denied at trial, the pair of staff members contacted the state teacher certification office and gave the impression that the alleged victim was prepared to testify against Doe. As a result of the staff members' response, the dean of the school of education refused to sign the required moral character form in support of his teacher certification application, concluding that there was "sufficient evidence of a serious behavioral problem" (p. 395). Without said form, Doe was unable to obtain a teaching certificate from the state.

Doe sued the university, the two staff members, and the persons whom they had cited as sources of information. His claims were for various common law torts, including defamation and negligent investigation, and for violation of the nondisclosure provision of FERPA. A state court jury returned a verdict in Doe's favor for $855,000 in compensatory damages and $300,000 in punitive damages. The compensatory damages included $500,000 for defamation, $100,000 for invasion of privacy, and $50,000 for negligence. The FERPA claim accounted for $150,000 of the compensatory damages and the $300,000 in punitive damages.

Washington's Supreme Court ultimately upheld the verdict, except for the $50,000 attributable to the negligence claim. Upon the university's subsequent appeal to the U.S. Supreme Court for the federal, i.e., FERPA, issue, the nation's highest court ruled that FERPA—which only provides for enforcement via a complaint process within the U.S. Department of Education—does not provide for an individual's right to sue, thus reversing the $150,000 of compensatory damages and the $300,000 of punitive damages attributable to this federal statute.

In the final case in this subcategory, a student teacher filed suit against a local school district in the wake of his dismissal from student teaching (*Cornell v. Pleasant Grove Independent School District*, 2005). The basis for the school district's dismissal action was the student teacher's belated admission of a prior felony in another state. Cornell alleged that the district also shared this information with a third party. Proceeding *pro se,* Cornell sued for $300,000, claiming that the school district's actions had damaged his reputation, caused personal humiliation and mental anguish, and led to loss of future employment. He also claimed violation of his civil rights. The defendant school district moved for a more specific statement of the charges, contending that the initial complaint was so vague and ambiguous that the district could not provide the requisite response. The court agreed and gave the student teacher additional time to re-plead the case. When Cornell failed to do so, the court granted the defendant district's motion for dismissal, thus ending another attempt to sue without legal counsel.

Insubordination and Intemperance

For this subcategory, we include not only classic cases of insubordination in terms of deliberate refusal to obey a superior's reasonable directives but also noncompliance with the policy of the higher education institution or local school district. Overlapping therewith, we also include cases of confrontation with either superiors or other employees and other behaviors that may be broadly regarded as intemperance.

In the earliest court case in this subcategory, a federal trial court dismissed the constitutional claim of a group of college students that included but was not limited to student teachers (*Scott v. Alabama State Board of Education*, 1969). The state college had either suspended or dismissed approximately 50 students due to their participation in a demonstration that had caused the closing of the college. As a result, the participating student teachers lost their school placements. The college sent notice, listing the charges to each of the students, and held a hearing. At the hearing, the students' attorney objected to the charges as being unconstitutionally vague, but the hearing committee denied this request to make the charges more definite. Declining further participation in the hearings, the students filed suit in federal court, relying on not only Fourteenth Amendment procedural due process but also First Amendment freedom of expression.

The court rejected students' Fourteenth Amendment claim, concluding that even if one of the charges was vague, the rest were sufficiently specific to satisfy the "rudimentary element of fair play" (p. 166) that is the essence of constitutional due process. The court also summarily disposed of their First Amendment claim because the students' disruptive conduct, beyond their expressions of protest, was not protected speech.

Three decades later, Wayne Nickerson, a student teacher in a public university's graduate special education program, encountered difficulties with his host, or cooperating, teachers (*Nickerson v. University of Alaska*, 1999). The university's supervising faculty member met with him and warned him about the problem and, despite Nickerson's assurances that he had corrected it, offered his suggestions for improving his working relationships.

Nevertheless, the problem persisted; a couple of days later the principal sent the supervising faculty member an e-mail insisting that Nickerson had continually failed to accept the teachers' constructive criticism and follow their directives. His e-mail ended with the adamant admonition that "we won't let kids, teachers, or the system be compromised."

After consulting with the dean of the school of education, the faculty member notified Nickerson of the suspension of his placement pending an investigatory meeting between the school and university representatives. The meeting took place the next day, when the school representatives confirmed their conclusion that the situation had become unworkable. The faculty member promptly met with Nickerson to notify him of his removal from student teaching and followed up the next day with written confirmation, which included his right to appeal. It also included notification that the faculty member would be meeting with his special education colleagues to review Nickerson's status in the certification preparation program. After the meeting, in which the faculty members voted unanimously to dismiss Nickerson from the program, the dean notified him in writing of this decision for failure to meet the working-relationship standards of the student teaching handbook and, as specified in the university catalog, included Nickerson's right to appeal.

Nickerson filed an appeal with the university vice president, seeking reinstatement based on an alleged procedural violation of the handbook. At the meeting with the vice president, Nickerson explained his assertion that the meeting of the special education faculty without allowing him to be present was the alleged violation. The vice president denied his appeal, and Nickerson filed suit in state court.

The state trial court decided that the university had complied with the student teaching handbook and had not denied Nickerson due process, ordering him to pay $1,300 for part of the university's attorneys' fees. On appeal, the state's highest court agreed that the university had "substantially" (p. 51) followed the applicable steps in the handbook. Similarly reflecting deference to the university in what might be classified as a contractual case, the appellate court's response to Nickerson's second, alternative argument by concluding that the university had "reasonably" (p. 52) complied with the appeal procedures in its official catalog.

However, Nickerson's third, alternative argument—which was based on constitutional due process—was partially, or at least inconclusively, successful. Specifically, while declining to resolve whether a student has a property interest in continued enrollment in a graduate program, the court concluded that Nickerson's dismissal for "allegedly 'hostile,' 'abrasive,' 'intimidating,' and 'unprofessional' behavior sufficiently stigmatizes a person's professional reputation in a chosen career field to constitute an infringement of a liberty interest" (p. 52).

As the next step in the procedural due process analysis, the court gave the university the benefit of the doubt on the "close question" (p. 52) of whether Nickerson's dismissal was academic or disciplinary, thus triggering the less rigorous procedural protections of *Board of Curators v. Horowitz* (see Chapter I). Nevertheless, given the closeness of the question, the court interpreted *Horowitz* as requiring the university in such a mixed situation to provide a heightened standard for the content and timing of the notice. Specifically, the university must provide notice with specific warning of the deficiency and the possible consequence, and it must "precede the academic dismissal by a reasonable time so that a student has a reasonable opportunity to cure his or her deficient performance" (p. 53). The court found that the record was not complete enough to apply this standard, remanding the matter to the trial court for a determination, while commenting in dicta that it looked like the university might not have informed Nickerson of his possible dismissal sufficiently in advance of the faculty's decision.

In interpreting the significance of the *Nickerson* decision, the reader should bear in mind that the court's unusually pro-plaintiff interpretation of constitutional due process was based on a dismissal from the entire certification program, not his removal from student teaching specifically. Additionally, although different from the prevailing trend, Nickerson's victory was inconclusive.

Three years later, another student teacher experienced a typical judicial outcome in *Swift v. Siesel* (2002). The school district superintendent had dismissed Chantell Swift from her student teaching assignment after she had slapped a substitute teacher's face in a room full of elementary school students. Police arrested and charged her with battery. After investigating the incident, the district officials barred her from student teaching in the school district. She sued the school officials and the school board, claiming violation of Fourteenth Amendment rights and breach of contract.

First, the federal trial judge rejected Swift's procedural due process claim, reasoning that she, as a "non-employee," had no protected property right in continued "employment" at the public school (p. *7). As a student, the court concluded, she "had a constitutional property interest in a public education..." (p. *9) but not to student teach at a particular school. Thus, Swift was not entitled to a hearing before her dismissal from student teaching. Second and similarly, the judge made short shrift of the Swift's substantive due process claim, concluding the school had reasonably based its decision on the evidence on record. Finally, the court summarily disposed of Swift's breach of contract claim, concluding that she was not a party or even a third-party beneficiary of any contract between the school and the University that the student teaching handbook may have created.

More recently, the constitutional claims of a former student teacher were at trial (*Leone v. Whitford,* 2007/2008). Diane Leone was an art major at a public university who applied to the college of education, resulting in contingent admissions based on her previous pattern of confrontational conduct, misrepresentation, and threatening messages to university staff members. Specifically, the dean admitted her with a warning of removal from the program if she displayed confrontational behavior. On the tenth day of student teaching, which was required for the B.S. in art education with state teacher certification, Leone ripped down the bulletin board she had been working on after the cooperating teacher suggested changes. A week later, a special university committee held a hearing with her concerning the incident. The resulting decision was to withdraw her from the student teaching placement and the certification program and to offer her the opportunity to work on the department's web page as an independent study project to fulfill the B.S. degree in art education with no certification.

Leone worked on the independent study project but refused to fill out the application for the alternative degree program, insisting instead on another opportunity for student teaching and claiming that the university had misappropriated her intellectual property by posting her independent study work on the website. When the department denied her request, she called the dean at home. The dean, who viewed the conversation as threatening and frightening, reported the call to the police and revoked her admission to the college.

After her appeal within the university was unsuccessful, Leone sued in federal court, alleging violations of both the federal Constitution, e.g., Fourteenth Amendment substantive and procedural due process, and state common law, e.g., slander and intentional infliction of emotional distress. The federal district court granted the defendant-university's motion for summary judgment.

First, the judge rejected the substantive due process claim, concluding that Leone had no fundamental right to a university degree with a recommendation for certification or clear entitlement to the degree and, in any event, the university's actions did not constitute the requisite substantial departure from accepted academic norms. Second, the judge concluded that Leone's art department advisor's alleged assurance that she could obtain the desired B.S. without completing student teaching did not create the requisite state law entitlement for procedural due process. Third, the judge summarily rejected her Fifth Amendment claims regarding the alleged appropriation of her intellectual property because she had not exhausted the available state remedies. Finally, the court declined to exercise discretionary, supplemental jurisdiction for her common law claims.

Upon Leone's appeal, the Second Circuit Court of Appeals summarily affirmed the lower court's decision. Leone's Fifth Amendment claim was the only one that the appellate court addressed, and the appellate court made short shrift of it based on both the exhaustion doctrine and, alternatively, the claim's lack of merit.

In another recent case (*Snyder v. Millersville University,* 2008), Snyder started her student teaching at a local high school. Within a few months, she was teaching a full load of courses and referring to the pupils in those classes as "my students." In her mid-placement evaluation, her supervising professor evaluated her work on two separate forms, one from the university and the other from the state education department. He rated her overall performance as "satisfactory." For the specific components, he reported that the student teacher had shown "good" or "reasonable" progress in most professionalism categories but needed to work on appropriate communications with others—including students, supervisors, and cooperating teachers—and establishing "proper teacher-student boundaries." Snyder's cooperating teacher's assessment was similar. While noting that Snyder had made "reasonable" or "good" professional progress, she expressed concern that Snyder had shared personal information with the students and needed "significant remediation" in other areas including preparation, performance, and student learning.

Contrary to the feedback from the supervising professor and cooperating teacher, Snyder continued to communicate with her students about personal matters via her MySpace webpage. For example, she posted a message apparently referring to her cooperating teacher as "the problem." She also put on her webpage a photograph of herself drinking along with the caption "drunken pirate."

Upon learning about these two postings, the cooperating teacher informed the school's administrators of the student teacher's actions. In turn, they notified the superintendent of their conclusions that Snyder (1) had disobeyed the cooperating teacher by communicating about personal matters with her students through her webpage; (2) had acted unprofessionally by criticizing the cooperating teacher to her students in the posting; and (3) had otherwise performed incompetently as a student teacher. The superintendent barred the student teacher from campus. In an attempt to improve the situation, Snyder wrote an error-filled apology to the cooperating teacher, school administrators, and supervising professor, which asked for forgiveness but—due to the many grammatical errors—sealed her fate.

Subsequently, the cooperating teacher and her supervising professor evaluated Snyder's professionalism as unsatisfactory. As a result, Snyder did not graduate with a degree in secondary education; instead the university granted her a B.A. in English. She unsuccessfully appealed to the dean and then to the academic vice president.

Snyder subsequently sued the university and its administrators in federal court, claiming a violation of her First Amendment freedom of speech. The relief that she sought was an injunction ordering the university to award her a degree in secondary education and to take the necessary steps to ensure her state teacher certification.

After a two-day nonjury trial, the judge decided in favor of the university defendants on two alternative grounds. First, the court explained that Snyder's requested injunctive relief claim was untenable in any event because the university did not have the authority to award the student teacher a degree in secondary education in the absence of her successful completion of required student teaching. Inasmuch as this completion was also a requirement for certification, the judge commented that Snyder's "proposed deception of the Pennsylvania Department of Education would 'disserve the public interest' and, thus, would be an impermissible abuse of this Court's equitable powers" (p. *24).

Second, finding the plaintiff's role as a student teacher at the high school "akin to that of a public employee" (p. *25), the judge used the three-step test for public employment expression rather than the framework that applies to public postsecondary student expression under the First Amendment. Snyder did not make it past the first step; the court concluded that her MySpace posting touched on purely personal matters rather than matters of public concern. Thus, the court did not have to proceed to the second and third steps of this flowchart-like analysis. Concluding that the First Amendment did not protect the expression at issue, the judge disposed of Snyder's suit, observing that "the federal court is not the appropriate forum in which to review the wisdom of a personnel decision taken when a public employee speaks upon matters of a personal interest" (p. *27).

Finally, another recent First Amendment case was unusual because although the student challenged the termination of her student teaching internship, she subsequently completed student teaching during a second internship and did not sue the university officials until after securing her degree, certification, and a teaching position in special education. In *Miller v. Houston County Board of Education* (2008), one member of the faculty committee that needed to approve of internship assignments expressed reservations about Miller's willingness to receive and use corrective feedback. Nevertheless, the district hired her for a special education vacancy that it had not been able to fill. She worked and received pay on the basis of a substitute teacher certificate. The university agreed to supervise this position as her required student teaching internship.

Approximately two months after this internship started, the university terminated it based on a continuing conflict between Miller and both the teachers and administrators in the Houston school system. She continued to assert that they were violating the legal rights of her special education students to the point that she left the building without permission in the middle of the day to register her concerns with one of the central administrators. Her coworkers claimed that she did not constructively accept feedback, lost control of her emotions in school, and lacked collegial cooperation. After the first month's observation, her university supervisor gave her an unsatisfactory rating. When the district personnel reported persisting problems with Miller's performance, he notified her that the internship was terminated with a grade of Incomplete. She subsequently completed student teaching at another school, where after graduating with her degree and certification, she obtained employment as a special education teacher. However, the position only lasted one year.

Miller filed suit in federal court, claiming that the school district had violated her First Amendment freedom of expression. She sought reinstatement to the original position, back pay, and both compensatory and punitive damages. The court granted the district's motion for summary judgment, concluding that Miller failed at the first step of the applicable analysis for public employment under the First Amendment.

More specifically, citing the Supreme Court's decision in *Garcetti v. Ceballos* (see Chapter I), the court concluded that Miller had made her statements pursuant to her official duties and, thus, her statements did not have First Amendment protection. In this case, the characterization of the student teacher as an employee is not subject to question; her unusual, paid arrangement with the school district—as reflected in her choice of defendant—clearly put her in the employee category. As a matter of dicta, the court commented that she would have lost in any event at subsequent steps of the analysis; for example, the evidence was preponderant that the district would have terminated her regardless of her expression due to leaving campus without permission, which was clearly contrary to the student teaching handbook and district policy.

Incompetence

The general definition of incompetence is inability or ineptitude in relation to performance expectations. The cases in this broad subcategory include performance problems of student teachers in terms of subject matter, teaching methods, interpersonal communication, and workplace attitudes.

In the earliest published court decision on student teaching (*Miller v. Dailey,* 1902), California's highest court ruled in favor of a dismissed student teacher, ordering the defendant teacher training institution—then termed a "normal school"—to readmit him and allow him to re-take student teaching. The student teacher in this case had conformed to the rules of the institution and had not received any failures during student teaching until the faculty terminated him from both the course and the institution. Their reason for termination was their judgment that he was not capable of becoming an effective teacher. The court concluded that this action was arbitrary and capricious due to a) the lack of previous feedback of unsatisfactory performance, b) the rather relaxed requirements, in the then-applicable state law, for participation in student teaching, and c) the past practice of allowing other students who had failed student teaching to take it a second time.

Separated by almost eight decades, *Aubuchon v. Olsen* (1979) was more representative of pertinent modern case law, with the outcome being judicial rejection of a student teacher's constitutional claims. The university, which as a public institution and thus subject to constitutional claims, had assigned John Aubuchon to a local high school for student teaching. After a month or so, he had performance problems, including failure to follow lesson plans and interfering with the cooperating teacher's grading of students. The vice principal held a meeting to discuss the problems with Aubuchon, the university supervisor, and the cooperating teacher. Aubuchon was uncooperative, refusing to tell his side of the story. After the meeting, the vice principal told him not to return to the school. The university supervisor wrote a note to the dean, informing him about the meeting and hinting that Aubuchon might have emotional illness. The college dean provided Aubuchon with notice of the performance charges, and he declined the dean's offer for a meeting.

After graduating from the university without receiving teacher certification, Aubuchon filed suit in federal court, claiming a violation of Fourteenth Amendment due process. The court dismissed the procedural due process claim based on lack of prerequisite property or liberty interest. Specifically focusing on Aubuchon's asserted liberty interest, the court cited the Supreme Court's decision in *Board of Curators v. Horowitz* (see Chapter I) for the rule that "absent a stigma to plaintiff's good name or reputation . . . , a decision to dismiss a student for failure to attain academic standards will not be disturbed by the courts unless there is evidence of arbitrary action or bad faith" (p. 572). Aubuchon asserted that the professor's note to the dean provided the requisite stigma. However, the court found that the note was not the basis of the dean's decision and that there was no evidence that the university would reveal its contents to any other universities to which Aubuchon might seek admission.

Alternatively, the court also rejected Aubuchon's assertion, under the *Horowitz* standard, that the decision was arbitrary or in bad faith. The court concluded that instead—with obvious deference to the school and university representatives—the facts clearly supported the reason for the termination decision. Effectively nailing the door shut, the court concluded that even if one were to assume for the sake of argument that Aubuchon was entitled to a hearing, the meeting in the assistant principal's office was "all that due process required" (p. 573).

A few years later, another court rejected a similar constitutional claim in *Hoffman v. Grove* (1983). In this case, after initially observing the student teacher's classroom instruction, the public university's supervisor developed a list of particulars that needed improvement, such as correct grading of papers, spelling on the blackboard, and management of the classroom. After the third observation, the university supervisor informed Hoffman of his dismissal from his student teaching placement due to his failure to improve, but offered him the option of attempting his student teaching experience in another school during the following semester.

Instead of utilizing the university's grievance procedure, Hoffman sued the university and school district representatives, alleging they had violated his right to procedural due process under the Fourteenth Amendment. In a brief, two-page decision, the court concluded the student teacher's procedural due process claim had no foundation due to the exhaustion doctrine, i.e., Hoffman had not utilized the available grievance procedure. In dicta, the court pointed out (1) the apparent absence of the requisite denial of a property or liberty interest, inasmuch his dismissal was from student teaching, not from the college or even the certification program, and (2) the notice and opportunity for a hearing that he had received in any event.

More than a decade later, another student teacher's constitutional claim resulted in a similar verdict in *Lucas v. Hahn* (1994). A dispute over grades arose when student teacher John Lucas sent letters to the cooperating teacher and the affected students alleging that the cooperating teacher had wrongfully lowered many of his tentative grades. After holding a meeting to discuss the incident, the college's education department representatives informed Lucas of his termination from the certification program due to his failure to comply with the student teaching handbook provisions pertaining to confidentiality of personally identifiable information and compliance with host school policies. However, they allowed him to remain in the Master's degree program in education.

To no avail, Lucas appealed the termination decision to the successive levels of the college up to the president. During this process, he made numerous requests for documents. The college officials provided him with some of the requested documents and notified him that the rest no longer existed or were otherwise unavailable. He sued in state court, alleging violation of Vermont's Access to Public Records Act and Fourteenth Amendment due process. The school officials successfully filed a motion for summary judgment, and he appealed.

First, the state's supreme court made short shrift of Lucas's constitutional claim. More specifically, the court concluded that the college had afforded the student teacher "at least as much due process as the Fourteenth Amendment requires," because his removal from the program was "an academic decision"

(p. 458). The court explained that concerns about a student teacher's "ability to adhere to ethical standards and to cooperate with superiors in the school setting . . . [in] the context of the licensure program . . . are valid academic matters; because they rank as important measures of an individual's ability to perform as a teacher" (p. 458). Thus, the college providing the student teacher with adequate pre-deprivation notice and an opportunity to be heard was all the procedural process that was due. Similarly, the court rejected his claim of alleged violations of the state open records act, concluding the college discharged its obligations to the student teacher, and attempted to meet "reasonable requests in good faith" (p. 460).

A year later, in *Banks v. Dominican College* (1995), a California appellate court not only rejected a student teacher's claims against the private college and school district but also ordered her to pay $15,000 for court costs and part of the defendants' attorneys' fees. After successfully completing an undergraduate major in legal studies at the college, Banks enrolled in the college's graduate teacher certification program. During the clinical phase of her graduate program, which amounted to student teaching, at an elementary school, she exhibited erratic and sometimes disturbing episodes of unprofessional behavior. For instance, she repeatedly left her second-grade students unattended, was inappropriately harsh with them, evidenced difficulty maintaining order in the classroom, and failed to properly perform many routine teaching duties. After her problems continued unabated despite counseling and advice, the college—with the strong recommendation and support of the school district—terminated her from student teaching, whereupon she did not graduate. She utilized the college's grievance procedure, but to no avail.

Claiming a vast conspiracy against her, Banks sued the college and the school district for a) breach of contract, b) breach of the covenant of good faith and fair dealing, c) intentional or negligent interference with prospective economic advantage, d) defamation, and e) intentional or negligent infliction of emotional distress. After five years of unsuccessful litigation, including the termination or withdrawal of five different attorneys for the student teacher and her ultimately representing herself, the trial court eventually granted summary judgment to the college.

Upon Banks' appeal, the appellate court agreed with the trial court that she had no factual basis for her various claims. For example, the appeals court observed that she had not presented any evidence of outrageous conduct on the college's or the district's part, which is an essential element for intentional infliction of emotional distress. Rather, the court reasoned that the district "had a responsibility to its students to remove [her] from a classroom when it concluded, in good faith and based on probable cause, that her continued disturbing presence was not in the best interests of its students" (p. 116). Finally, the court ordered Banks to pay $7,500 to each of the two defendant institutions and $2,000 for court costs due to a frivolous appeal. The court explained that the monetary sanctions were warranted under state law because the student teacher had a) presented arguments that were totally without merit and frivolous, b) abused the legal system, and c) caused the defendants to "suffer large expenses which would have been better spent for beneficial educational purposes" (p. 120).

In the final case in this subcategory, a student teacher was unsuccessful in his First and Fourteenth Amendment claims (*Hennessy v. City of Melrose,* 1999). As part of his teacher education program at a state college, Robert Hennessy started his student teaching with satisfactory performance. However, a few months later, three incidents arose revealing that his strong Christian beliefs stood above his responsibilities as a student teacher. For example, he grudgingly—only when his cooperating teacher made the request a directive—attended the school's multicultural "Family Fiesta," left immediately, and openly objected to activities as offensive to the principles of "biblical sobriety." The fourth and final incident occurred when the principal called him to inquire about the previous events. During the meeting, Hennessy called the principal "the devil" (p. 243) and persisted in arguing against the alleged denigration of religion in the school curriculum. Moreover, he refused when she instructed him to meet with the superintendent.

Citing the four incidents that were contrary to the student teaching handbook, the principal informed the college supervisor that she would not allow Hennessy to continue student teaching at her school. The college temporarily suspended Hennessy and notified him that he was entitled to an immediate hearing. However, upon learning that the principal would not testify at the hearing, the college officials dropped the disciplinary proceedings and rescinded the temporary suspension. Hennessy received a failing grade in his teaching assignment because he failed to meet four of the common teaching competencies—communication skills, self-evaluation, equity, and professionalism—that the state required for teaching certification.

Hennessy filed suit against both the college and the district, claiming a violation of his First Amendment expression and Fourteenth Amendment due process. The federal trial court granted the defendants' motion for summary judgment. Hennessy appealed. The First Circuit Court of Appeals affirmed the lower court's decision.

First, the appellate court rejected Hennessy's First Amendment speech claim. Finding the "apprentice-type" relationship to more closely approximate the employee than the student relationship, the court used the three-step test for public employment expression rather than the framework that applies to public student expression. At the first step, the appellate court concluded that student teacher's expression during the four incidents was at least partially a matter of public concern, thus warranting a balancing of interests. Doing so, the court determined that "the school's strong interest in preserving a collegial atmosphere, harmonious relations among teachers, and respect for the curriculum while in the classroom outweighed the [student teacher's] interest in proselytizing for his chosen cause" (p. 247).

As an incidental note, the court made short shrift of Hennessy's overlapping free exercise claim, concluding that, "to whatever extent [Hennessy's] actions were dictated by his religious beliefs, those beliefs do not excuse him as an apprentice teacher in the public school system from complying with the legislative mandate and implementing the designated curriculum" (p. 244 n.1).

Finally, for procedural due process under Fourteenth Amendment, the court questioned whether the university had deprived Hennessy of a property or liberty interest. The court declined to decide this issue, because in any event the college's action was academic, rather than disciplinary, thus not requiring a hearing based on applicable Supreme Court precedent (see Chapter I–*Board of Curators v. Horowitz*).

The First Circuit explained this determination in two ways. The academic nature was obvious first in the inevitably subjective assessment of his performance; in light of state's requirement for certification, Hennessy's inability to communicate effectively with his colleagues and his unwillingness to work "reasonably" within the prescribed curriculum were as important, "from an academic standpoint, as his ability to prepare a lesson plan" (p. 250). As for the abortive disciplinary decision, the court found no evidence that the basis was anything other than "the faculty's academic judgment that [Hennessy] had neither completed the required assignments nor demonstrated the practical qualities necessary to perform efficaciously as a public school teacher" (p. 251).

As for substantive due process, the court cited the pertinent precedent (see Chapter I–*Regents v. Ewing*) to conclude:

> [Hennessy] has adduced no evidence from which we could infer that [the college's] decision was "beyond the pale of reasoned academic decision making." . . . Although [the college] could have opted for a different course (e.g., it might have tried to transfer Hennessy to another elementary school to finish his practicum), the course it chose was a reasonable solution to a vexing set of circumstances. In the usual case, courts should leave such judgment calls to the academicians-and this case falls comfortably within the mine-run (p. 252).

Wrongful Evaluation

This catchall subcategory includes seven cases that were difficult to fit in the other, more specific subcategories, due in large part to insufficient information in the court opinions. In many of these cases, the focus was on adjudicative or other procedures, thus not necessitating factual details including the specific grounds for dismissal. However, in all these cases the plaintiff student teachers contended that their dismissal was based on a wrongful evaluation of their performance.

In an early and outlier decision, a dismissed student teacher prevailed on a constitutional claim (*Moore v. Gaston County Board of Education*, 1973). For the first three months of his student teaching, George Moore performed his duties well. Trouble arose when one day he substituted for one of the teachers. During the discussion in a class on the history of religion in the Middle East, Moore gave relatively reserved agnostic answers to students' questions about creation, evolution, immortality, and the nature and existence of God. After receiving heated complaints from parents, the superintendent arranged a quick meeting with Moore, inquired only about the previous day's statements, and—after Moore's effective admission but without an opportunity for any explanation or any other effort of investigation—dismissed him from the student teaching placement.

Moore filed suit in federal court on various constitutional grounds. The federal trial court decided in Moore's favor on three separate bases. First, the judge sided with Moore on the First Amendment claim, concluding that the balance between the plaintiff's interest in academic freedom and the public school's interest in protecting impressionable minds lies in school officials providing the educator with adequate notice of the boundaries between permissible and impermissible expression. Here, the court concluded that "we are concerned not merely with vague standards, but with the total absence of standards" (p. 1041), thereby having the unconstitutional result of the unfettered discretion of school officials to censor or censure expression.

Second, the court agreed with Moore's Fourteenth Amendment procedural due process claim, concluding—in contrast with the earlier *Rowe* decision—that he had a reasonable expectation, i.e., property right, to continue his student teaching. Interpreting student teachers as having the same protection as certified teachers regardless of compensation or tenure under applicable state law, the court concluded that the school district had deprived the plaintiff of this property right via a "hearing with twenty minutes notice before a hostile ad hoc committee without eyewitness testimony" and with the questioning focused on a few "unorthodox statements" (p. 1042).

Third, the court concluded that the district decision to discharge a teacher—which the court found was Moore's status under North Carolina legislation—without warning because "his answers to scientific and theological questions do not fit the notions of the local parents and teachers" (p. 1043) is a violation of the First Amendment's establishment clause.

Readers are cautioned not to over-rely on Moore's victory. As explained in Chapter I, the more recent judicial trends have largely moved in the defendants' direction. First, if indeed a student teacher fits the status of teacher for the purpose of First Amendment expression, the modern multi-step test—which subsumes the concept of academic freedom—would likely lead to the opposite outcome. Indeed, Moore would probably not hurdle the initial step of threshold protection based on the Supreme Court's recent ruling in *Garcetti v. Ceballos* (2006). Second, the interpretation and application of the First Amendment's religion clauses—not only establishment but also free exercise—have been more fluid and, thus, uncertain, but are not clearly in favor of Moore. Finally, although the property right for Fourteenth Amendment purposes varies depending on the specific nature of student teaching and the different contours of state law, the odds—as demonstrated in not only the earlier *Rowe* decision and the subsequent *Swift* decision—would not be in Moore's favor, and in any event a court might conclude that Moore received all of the process to which he was due.

Several years later, a federal court judge dismissed a student teacher's lawsuit because he filed suit too late, i.e., beyond the statute of limitations *(Arko v. U.S. Air Force Reserve Officer Training Program* 1987). Proceeding *pro se,* i.e., without a lawyer, against multiple defendants twenty years after the challenged actions, the plaintiff sought to challenge not only his expulsion from the school of education's student teaching program but also his purportedly forced withdrawal from the Air Force Reserve Training Program and the subsequent denial of his two successive admission applications for attending law school, all at the University of Colorado. Inasmuch as the defendants, including the university, were public institutions, his primary claims were based on the Constitution, specifically Fourteenth Amendment due process and equal protection. However, he never had his day in court, because the judge granted the defendants' motion due to the statute of limitations that applied to each claim. Thus, proceeding without legal counsel and otherwise not being diligent contributed to an abortive resort to litigation.

A few years later, a student teacher appealed a lower court's decision in favor of the university and suffered a similar losing fate (*Embrey v. Central State University,* 1991). Ernestine Embrey had enrolled in the student teaching course for a second time after her first attempt was unsuccessful due to deficient performance. When her second try resulted in another grade of "F," Embrey sued the university, claiming that the supervising faculty member's failure to provide her with written evaluations prior to her course grade constituted a breach of contract.

Affirming the trial court's rejection of Embrey's claim, the appellate court examined the applicable university documents for student teaching, finding only a policy for oral conferences or consultations. Thus, the court concluded that the university had not committed breach of contract. Additionally, the court observed that both sides had been remiss—the student for not inquiring whether her performance had improved since her previous deficient attempt and the supervising faculty member for only communicating her concerns with the cooperating classroom teacher, not with the student teacher. Nevertheless, any breach was not material because the university had fully advised the student of the specific performance criteria, and she had failed to fulfill them. The bottom-line deference to academic discretion was obvious in the disposition of this case.

Three years later, student teacher William Rust sued not only the university but also the faculty member who was the supervisor for student teaching, claiming that the supervisor had wrongfully evaluated his performance, resulting in his dismissal from the program and other injuries (*Rust v. Tufts University*, 1994). His tort claims included defamation and intentional infliction of emotional distress, and his additional claim was breach of contract. The individual, not the institutional, defendant was the focus of this court decision. Specifically, the supervising faculty member filed a motion for dismissal, and the court granted it. First, the breach of contract claim failed because the university, not the faculty member, was the contracting party. Second, the fatal flaw in Rust's tort claims, including defamation, was that he admitted in his pleadings that he did not have the necessary skills to be a teacher, thus contradicting his assertion that the faculty member misrepresented his performance.

Several years later, after Indria Bulloch graduated with a degree in education but without teacher certification, she sued the university for breach of contract, claiming that the "W" on her transcript for student teaching and the consequent refusal to recommend her for certification violated the student-institution contract (*Bulloch v. State*, 2002). The state trial court decided in favor of the university, concluding that Bulloch had not fulfilled her side of the agreement by not successfully completing student teaching. Noting its previous dismissal of Bulloch's alternate claim of intentional infliction of emotional distress due to her failure to provide the requisite notice to the defendant, the court's three overlapping conclusions also firmly shut the door on her contractual claim.

First, the *Bulloch* court followed the general judicial doctrine of deferring to the academic decisions of university, explaining that "the educational contract between the student and the educational institution inherently and implicitly adopts the academic standards of the institution—including subjective or academic standards" (p. *2), concluding that such matters are properly within the expertise of the university, not the court.

Second, the court cited the testimony of the supervising teachers that Bulloch had demonstrated various performance problems that did not improve after feedback. The only rebuttal that Bulloch offered was her own opinion, which the court regarded as "neither fully competent nor persuasive" (p. *3).

Finally, the court addressed Bulloch's undisputed claim that the university transcript listed for student teaching a "W," indicating withdrawal, whereas she had not officially withdrawn from the course. Observing that the university had not opted to follow the supervising teacher's recommendation that she receive a failing grade, the court did not side with the student but included a message for the university in characterizing its unilateral action as a "generous and gentle, but thankless decision to mismark claimant's academic record with a benign W in lieu of the scarlet-like F—quite obviously done to avoid stigmatizing her in her chosen profession despite her inadequate performance that semester, and in the process treaded close to academic dishonesty" (p. *4).

One year later, the Sixth Circuit affirmed the summary rejection of Douglas Hutchings' suit against a private university that had removed him from student teaching less unilaterally (*Hutchings v. Vanderbilt University*, 2003). The university offered, and he accepted, the option to switch from teacher education to education studies, thus leading to his graduation but lack of teacher certification. He filed suit in federal court, initially alleging sex discrimination under Title IX, violation of his First Amendment right to expression, and various state law claims, including negligence and breach of contract. However, he eventually abandoned all of the claims except these last two, asserting that the university had failed to provide adequate educational services during his two successive student teaching assignments. The appellate court agreed with the lower court that both Hutchings' negligence and contractual claims did not amount to educational malpractice, which modern precedents have generally rejected on policy grounds, including academic abstention (i.e., judicial principle of particularly strong deference to defendant-school for issues of educational expertise).

In the most recent case in this subcategory, *Burns v. Slippery Rock University* (2007), the university removed the student teacher from her field experience based on the recommendation of the cooperating district soon after the start of her assignment. After Stephanie Burns graduated with a degree but no certification in elementary education, she sued both the university and the school district under Section 504 and the ADA, claiming the reason for the removal was her disability in hearing and speaking.

In response to the defendants' motion for summary judgment, the court initially rejected the suit, concluding that Burns had failed to show that she met the definition of disability under these two federal disability discrimination statutes. However, upon Burns' motion for reconsideration, the court reversed its decision, thus preserving the matter for trial. The reason was the court's conclusion that although the plaintiff fell fatally short of showing that her hearing and speech impairments were substantial limitations, her allegations were sufficient for a trial as to whether the defendants regarded her as having such a limitation, which is an alternative prong of the Section 504 and ADA definition of disability (see Chapter I).

Although—by way of contrast—Burns survived to the next stage of the litigation, her victory was limited and inconclusive. Under the recent ADA Amendments, which—as noted in Chapter I—expanded the definitional standards for the scope of "disability" under both Section 504 and the ADA, Burns would have increased odds of prevailing at this initial hurdle, but she would still have the burden to prove that the university failed to provide her with reasonable accommodations. In turn, the university would argue that even with such accommodations, she would not have met the performance standards for student teaching and that any additional necessary accommodations would constitute either undue fiscal hardship or fundamental alteration. Thus, the outcome is an open question, but this latest case reflects the relatively recent rise of disability discrimination claims.

TAXATION ISSUES FOR STUDENT TEACHING

The fourth and final category consists of a small series of tax court cases specific to student teachers in special programs that provided a stipend or tuition benefits, which IRS taxed and which the student teacher challenged in tax court. Even interpreting student teaching rather broadly to extend to various school-related internships, although not so far as higher education teaching as part of a regular graduate assistantship (*Russell v. Commissioner of Internal Revenue*, 1987), the line of cases is relatively limited. In each case, unlike the general trend for student teaching, the plaintiff participated in a special program that included payment as part of the student teaching. The other commonality of this special category of cases is that they all were based on interpreting the provision in the income tax code that excluded scholarship or fellowship grants except for those that required part-time employment as a condition of the grant.

In the first case, which was in the mid-1960s, a candidate for a Master of Arts in Teaching (M.A.T.) sought to exclude from her gross income the $1,900 she received from the school board for the one-semester intern teaching assignment that she performed as a required part of the M.A.T. program *(Reese v. Commissioner of Internal Revenue*, 1966/1967). This assignment was different from the ordinary, undergraduate student teaching program because the student took full responsibility for the classroom. The $1,900 for the half year was based on the salary scale for a teacher with a bachelor's degree but without a teaching certificate. She also received a Ford Foundation scholarship in the form of tuition remission of $1,200, but the excludability of that amount was not at issue in this case. The tax court determined that although the applicable provision of the tax code was not crystal clear, the amount at issue was taxable. The Fourth Circuit Court of Appeals affirmed the tax court's decision without further opinion.

In the same year, another student challenged the IRS's taxing of not only the stipend that she received but also the educational expenses that she incurred for a special internship program to become a high school guidance counselor (*Schwerm v. Commissioner of Internal Revenue*, 1966).[3] Under this program, which the Wisconsin state education department implemented through five state universities, the internship was the extension, i.e., directly after the completion, of a master's degree in school counseling. The one-year internship was full-time for one year, with escalating duties but without replacement of any regular counselor in the participating district. The district paid the participant approximately 60% of a beginning counselor's salary from funds received from her sponsoring state university. In addition, the intern who was the plaintiff in this case had incurred almost $2,000 in educational expenses, including tuition and the costs of attending a training conference during the year in question.

The tax court ruled that Schwerm's internship program stipend was in the nature of a scholarship or fellowship grant but that the exclusion was subject to the limitation—then $300 per month—applicable to taxpayers who are not candidates for degrees. The court also ruled that Schwerm's educational expenses were deductible because (1) they improved her skills in, without being necessary to meet the minimum requirements for, her former position, which was a discussion leader in an adult education program, and (2) the succeeding positions of intern and counselor were the same type of work rather than being a new trade or business.

In an even more marginally relevant case in 1974, a husband and wife who participated in an externally funded project designed to prepare teachers in community colleges and postsecondary vo-tech schools similarly sought to exclude the amount that they had received for the one-semester intern teaching component (*Abrams v. Commissioner of Internal Revenue*, 1974). Each intern in this special program taught two community college classes under the supervision of a master teacher, who received a one-class reduction in teaching load for this purpose. Each intern also participated in various activities as the remainder of this 12-credit semester, and they received stipends ranging from approximately $1,500 to $4,000, depending on whether they had prior experience in the discipline taught and whether they were in the Master's degree program. Based on the various features of this special program, the tax court concluded that the amounts these two participants had received met the characteristics associated with a scholarship and, thus, were excludable from income.

Finally, another husband and wife both participated in a special program that the University of North Dakota, the state education department, and the state legislature established to upgrade the qualifications of elementary teachers, who were largely at the bachelor's degree level (*Bredahl v. Commissioner of Internal Revenue*, 1977). The couple in question received M.Ed. degrees in elementary education after taking the requisite courses and serving as intern teachers in a participating district. The district paid the university an amount approximating the salary of a new bachelor's-level teacher, and the university paid the candidate approximately 75% of that amount and also remitted their tuition and fees. Moreover, part of the agreement was that upon completion of the program the candidate would work as a teacher in the district for a period at least equal to that of the program. Citing its prior decision in *Reese*, the tax court concluded that these grants were "bargained for payments given by the [participating district] primarily as compensation in return for present or future services" (p. *9) and, thus, were not excludable as scholarships or fellowships.

Although included for the sake of completeness and to show the diversity of legal issues that have arisen for student teachers, these tax cases are of limited legal weight. They are clearly fact-specific and based on relatively unusual student teaching arrangements, and they are relatively old cases in a specialized and fluid area of law. Thus their "currency" is in question.

SUMMARY

Student teaching is a high-stakes enterprise, representing the culmination of a student's teacher preparation program and, for the university-approval route, the prerequisite to teacher certification. As the preceding chapter shows in more detail, legislation in each of the 50 states provides institutions of higher education with express or implied authority for this endeavor, often via interinstitutional agreements with school districts. On occasion, the representatives of the sponsoring institution of higher education or the cooperating school district make a decision that deprives college of education students of commencing or completing student teaching, which in some cases leads to litigation.

A review and analysis of the resulting published case law, including the charted results in Appendix B, yields some trends and useful considerations for student teachers and, conversely, for the participating institutions. First, both sides but particularly—in light of the difference between emotional knee-jerk inclinations and objectively likely outcomes—student teachers need to think carefully before proceeding with a lawsuit. The "costs" of litigation, including not only attorneys' fees and court costs but also the often underestimated time and adversariness, are considerable and draining. Moreover, as an examination of the Appendix B reveals, for the 38 cases where a student teacher sued the institution of higher education and/or the school district, the success rate was 4 (10%) outright wins and 3 (8%) inconclusive favorable decisions, i.e., surviving the initial hurdles to get to a trial. The student teacher lost entirely in the remaining 27 cases, representing an almost 4:1 odds of outright loss, and in a few of the cases the court ordered the student teacher to pay at least part of the defendant-institutions' attorneys' fees.

Moreover, the four outright wins, i.e., decisions conclusively in favor of plaintiff student teachers, during the past 30 years were largely outliers. None of them was during the past 30 years. The *Miller* case was the earliest in our sample, thus being way beyond the modern mainstream of the pertinent published decisions. The *Moore* decision was prior to the Supreme Court's precedent in *Garcetti* decision and, thus, as explained above, clearly questionable in terms of current law. The *Betts* decision was limited to worker's compensation under a particular state statute, thus not being particularly significant or generic. Finally, *Doe v. Gonzaga University* (2001/2002), was a mixed outcome, where the student teacher scored a partial victory for his common law claims in the lower appellate court but lost on the more generalizable FERPA claim at the Supreme Court.

The second consideration is recognizing the significant legal difference between private and public institutions, because—as Appendix B shows—constitutional claims constitute the most common category for plaintiff student teachers, and such claims only apply to governmental institutions, such as local school districts and public universities.

The third and overlapping consideration is that—as Chapter I established—the courts have swung in recent years in favor of the defendant public educational institutions for these constitutional claims. Appendix B reveals that the most frequent bases of decision within the constitutional category are Fourteenth Amendment procedural or substantive due process and First Amendment freedom of expression and that the modern trend strongly disfavors plaintiff student teachers.

A fourth and successively overlapping trend that this chapter and its accompanying appendix reveal is the resurgence of the traditional "deference" doctrine, especially but not exclusively for academic issues. This trend is marked by judicial latitude for the expertise and discretion of educators, whether in public or private and at K–12 or higher education institutions.

A fifth consideration, which the summaries in this chapter show to be a repeating theme, is the tendency of student teachers to sue *pro se,* i.e., without legal counsel. Although as a person above the age of majority, a student teacher generally has the option to proceed *pro se* and although the limited economic means of the typical student teacher promotes selecting this option, the complexities of the applicable federal and state laws and the generally consistent outcomes of the *pro se* cases—sometimes at the threshold, pretrial stage based on adjudicative technicalities—would suggest thinking twice about this choice.

A sixth legal lesson is for institutions to have available and for student teachers to exhaust administrative remedies that provide for dispute resolution as an alternative to or at least precursor to litigation. The cases in this chapter illustrate the application of the exhaustion doctrine, which is illustrated in the first chapter and explained in the Glossary.

Finally, at a time when education litigation has remained relatively level overall, student teacher cases have accelerated in frequency; more than a third of the cases listed in Appendix B were decided during the past ten years. These recent cases identify some continuing and some new areas of legal concern.

More specifically, during this recent decade some of the student teachers' legal issues continue and without being clearly settled. For example, student teachers continue to have a hybrid but neither fish nor fowl status in terms of their higher education student and K–12 education employee status, depending on the context, the issue, and the jurisdiction. The most frequent examples of varying answers are First Amendment expression and state workers' compensation statutes.

Others are new and, thus, unsettling as well as unsettled. The leading example, accounting for two of the recent decisions, is the effect of Section 504 and the ADA on institutions of both K–12 and higher education, whether public or private. The primary and rather fluid interrelated questions in this context are: (1) is the student teacher eligible, in terms of the multi-pronged definition of disability under either or both of these statutes, and (2) did the defendant educational institution(s) provide the student teacher with reasonable accommodation—as compared with fundamental alterations or undue fiscal hardship?

In completing this chapter on the case law, the reader should take into consideration the other contents of this volume, which show the importance of state statutes, institutional policies, and the interaction with ethical and professional concerns. It is imperative not only to comply with minimum legal requirements but also—whether as a matter of preventive law or best practice—to optimize the procedural fairness and substantive effectiveness of programs that serve as the culminating step between being students in higher education and serving as teachers in our nation's K–12 schools. The profession of teaching and its noble mission for future of our nation's youth merit keeping law in its proper place.

References

Abrams v. Comm'r of Internal Revenue, 33 T.C.M. (CCH) 722 (Tax Ct. 1975).
Arbegast v. Bd. of Educ. of S. Berlin Cent. Sch., 490 N.Y.S.2d 751 (1985).
Arko v. U.S. Air Force Reserve Officer Training Program, 661 F. Supp. 31 (D. Colo. 1987).
Arrowhead United Teachers Org. v. Wisconsin Employment Relations Comm'n, 342 N.W.2d 709 (Wis. 1984).
Aubuchon v. Olsen, 467 F. Supp. 568 (E.D. Mo. 1979).
Banks v. Dominican Coll., 42 Cal. Rptr. 2d 110 (Ct. App. 1995).
Betts v. Ann Arbor Pub. Sch., 271 N.W.2d 498 (Mich. 1978).
Blanchard v. Keppel, 160 P. 690 (Cal. Ct. App. 1916).
Bd. of Curators of Univ. of Missouri v. Horowitz, 435 U.S. 78 (1978).
Bd. of Regents v. Roth, 408 U.S. 564 (1972).
Brahatcek v. Millard Sch. Dist., 273 N.W.2d 680 (Neb. 1979).
Bredahl v. Comm'r of Internal Revenue, 36 T.C.M. (CCH) 1474 (Tax Ct. 1977).
Brown v. Acorn Acres, Inc., 2000 WL 1337478 (Conn. Super. Ct. 2000).
Brown v. Bd. of Educ., 347 U.S. 483 (1954).
Bulloch v. State, 2002 WL 32705291 (Ill Ct. Cl. 2002).
Burns v. Slippery Rock Univ., 2007 WL 2317310 (W.D. Pa. 2007), *on reconsideration*, 2007 WL 2463402 (W.D. Pa. 2007).
Chouhoud, Y., & Zirkel, P. A. (2008). The *Goss* progeny: An empirical analysis. *San Diego Law Review, 45*, 353–382.
Clay v. Indep. Sch. Dist. of Cedar Falls, 174 N.W. 47 (Iowa 1919).
Cornell v. Pleasant Grove Indep. Sch. Dist., 2005 WL 2277396 (E.D. Tex. 2005).
D.R. v. Middle Bucks Area Vocational Technical Sch., 972 F.2d 1364 (3d Cir. 1992).
D'Angelo, A., & Zirkel, P. A. (2008). An outcomes analysis of student-initiated litigation. *West's Education Law Reporter, 226*, 539–555.
Dello v. State, 481 N.Y.S.2d 512 (App. Div. 1984).

DeMitchell, T. A. (1997). Teacher conduct outside the schoolhouse gate: Exemplar or nexus? *International Journal of Educational Reform, 6,* 91–96.
Doe v. Gonzaga Univ., 24 P.3d 390 (Wash. 2001), *rev'd on FERPA grounds sub nom. Gonzaga Univ. v. Doe,* 536 U.S. 273 (2002).
Donoso, S., Zirkel, P. A. (2008). The volume of higher education litigation: An updated analysis. *West's Education Law Reporter, 232,* 549–555."
Embrey v. Cent. State Univ., 1991 WL 224228 (Ohio Ct. App. 1991).
Everett v. Cobb County Sch. Dist., 138 F.3d 1407 (11th Cir. 1998).
Furlong v. Carroll Coll., 2001 Mont. Dist. LEXIS 1995 (Mont. Dist. Ct. 2001).
Garcetti v. Caballos, 547 U. S. 410 (2006).
Gardner v. State, 22 N.E.2d 344 (N. Y. 1939).
Gonzaga v. ..... see *Doe v. Gonzaga*
Goss v. Lopez, 419 U.S. 565 (1975).
Hall, G. C. (1990). *Legal relationship of student teachers to public institutions of higher education and public schools.* Unpublished doctoral dissertation, Indiana University.
Head v. Bd. of Trustees of Cal. St. Univ., 2007 Cal. App. Unpub. LEXIS 393 (Ct. App. 2007), *review denied,* 2007 Cal. LEXIS 3790 (2007), *federal proceedings,* 2006 U.S. Dist. LEXIS 60857 (C.D. Cal. 2006), *aff'd,* 2008 U.S. App. LEXIS 7590 (9th Cir. 2008).
Healy v. James, 408 U.S. 169 (1972).
Hennessy v. City of Melrose, 194 F.3d 237 (1st Cir. 1999).
Herschler, L. N. (2009). *The complete guide to student teaching.* Baltimore: Publish America.
Hoffman v. Grove, 301 S.E.2d 810 (W. Va. 1983).
Holt v. Munitz, 1996 WL 341430 (9th Cir. 1996).
Hunt v. Univ. of Alaska, 52 P.3d 739 (Alaska 2002).
Hutchings v. Vanderbilt Univ., 55 F. App'x. 308 (6th Cir. 2003). on the two lines after Hutchings, delete the repeated references to Garcetti and Gardner
James v. W. Virginia Bd. of Regents, 322 F. Supp. 217 (S.D. W. Va. 1971), *aff'd mem,* 448 F.3d 785 (4th Cir 1971).
Lai v. Bd. of Trustees of E. Carolina Univ., 330 F. Supp. 1037 (E.D.N.C. 1971).
Lee v. Weisman, 505 U.S. 577 (1992).
Leone v. Whitford, 2007 WL 11913472008 (D. Conn. 2007), *aff'd,* WL 4933841 (2d Cir. 2008).
Lindblad v. Bd. of Educ. of Normal Sch. Dist., 77 N.E. 450 (Ill. 1906).
Lucas v. Hahn, 648 A.2d 839 (Vt. 1994).
Mead, J. F., & Underwood, J. K. (1995). A legal primer for teachers. In G. Appelt (Ed.), *Emerging trends in teacher preparation: The future of field experiences* (pp. 43–51).Thousand Oaks, CA: Corwin Press.
Miller v. Dailey, 68 P. 1029 (Cal. 1902).
Miller v. Houston County Bd. of Educ., 2008 WL 696874 (M.D. Ala. 2008).
Moore v. Gaston County Bd. of Educ., 357 F. Supp. 1037 (W.D.N.C. 1973).
Morse v. Frederick, 551 U.S. 393 (2007).

Nickerson v. Univ. of Alaska, 975 P.2d 46 (Alaska 1999).
Orange County Sch. Bd. v. Powers, 959 So.2d 370 (Fla. Dist. Ct. App. 2007).
Perry v. Sindermann, 408 U.S. 593 (1972).
Reese v. Comm'r of Internal Revenue, 34 T.C. 407 (Tax Ct. 1966), aff'd mem., 373 F.2d 742 (4th Cir. 1967).
Regents of Univ. of Michigan v. Ewing, 474 U.S. 214 (1985).
Robinson v. Univ. of Miami, 100 So.2d 442 (Fla. Dist. Ct. App. 1958).
Rowe v. Chandler, 332 F. Supp. 335 (D. Kan. 1971).
Russell v. Comm'r of Internal Revenue, 53 T.C.M. (CCH) 692 (Tax Ct. 1987).
Rust v. Tufts Univ., 1994 WL 902984 (Mass. Super. Ct. 1994).
Safford Unified Sch. Dist. #1 v. Redding, 129 S. Ct. 2633 (2009).
Scott v. Alabama State Bd. of Educ., 300 F. Supp. 163 (M.D. Ala. 1969).
Schwerm v. Comm'r of Internal Revenue, 51 T.C.M. (CCH) 270 (Tax Ct. 1986).
Snyder v. Millersville Univ., 2008 WL 5093140 (E. D. Pa. 2008).
Spedden v. Bd. of Educ. of Indep. Sch. Dist. of Fairmont, 81 S.E. 724 (W. Va. 1914).
Stark v. St. Cloud State Univ., 802 F.2d 1046 (8th Cir. 1985).
Suppa, R., Skinner, C., & Zirkel, P. A. (1988). Conflict between ethical principles and legal protections for special services providers. *Special Services in the School, 5*, 153–161.
Swalls, F. (1976). *The law on student teaching in the United States*. Danville, IL: Interstate.
Swift v. Siesel, 2002 WL 1585617 (E.D. La. 2002).
Thomas v. Hamline Univ., 2008 WL 5071078 (D. Minn. 2008).
United States v. American Library Association, Inc., 539 U.S. 194 (2003).
Watson v. Connelly, 2008 WL 818939 (W.D. Pa. 2008).
Whitsel v. Se Local Sch. Dist., 484 F.2d 1222 (6th Cir. 1973).
Zirkel, P. A. (1998). National trends in education litigation: Supreme Court decisions concerning students. *Journal of Law & Education, 27*, 235–248.
Zirkel, P. A. (1999). The First Amendment and higher education students: The religion cases. *West's Education Law Reporter, 138*, 983–989.
Zirkel, P. A. (2001). Decisions that have shaped U.S. education. *Educational Leadership, 59*(2), 6–12.
Zirkel, P. A. (2005). A primer of special education law. *Teaching Exceptional Children, 38*(1), 62–63.
Zirkel, P. A. (2006a). Freedom of expression: An update. *Principal, 86*(2), 10–11.
Zirkel, P. A. (2006b). Paralyzing fear? Avoiding distorted assessments of the effect of law on education. *Journal of Law and Education, 35*, 461–496.
Zirkel, P. A. (2006c). Trends in law. In F. English (Ed.), *Encyclopedia of educational leadership and administration* (pp. 561–562). Thousand Oaks, CA: Sage.
Zirkel, P. A. (2007). The Supreme Court speaks on student expression: A revised map. *West's Education Law Reporter, 221*, 485–491.
Zirkel, P. A. (2009a). New Section 504 eligibility standards. *Teaching Exceptional Children, 41*(4), 68–71.
Zirkel, P. A. (2009b). School law all stars: Two successive constellations. *Phi Delta Kappan, 90*, 705–708.

Appendix A

State Statutory Chart

This chart, unlike the next one (i.e., Appendix B), is more illustrative than exhaustive. First, it does not include the statute regulations and policies that are explicitly or implicitly authorized by these statutes. Second, it does not extend to statutes that use terminology other than the search terms "student teacher" or "student teaching." Nevertheless, it provides a systematic synthesis, not available at all elsewhere in the literature, as to the variety of current—as of March 2009—state laws specific to student teachers and student teaching.

The successive column headings and citation entry (with parenthetical clarification) are as follows after the column containing the postal code abbreviations of the 50 states:

- Authorization—the enabling legislation that authorizes student teaching, in some cases with specific standards or by delegating such standards for state administrative regulations, designated as w. regs.
- Definitions—statutory definitions of student teacher, student teaching, and related terms
- ST Prerequisites—specification of minimum criteria for student teachers (ST)
- ST Authority—specification of role-type authority for student teachers (ST)
- ST Protection—specification of particular protections or immunities for student teachers (ST)
- Coop. Tchr.—specified duties, benefits, or processes for cooperating teachers
- Other—miscellaneous other notable provisions specific to student teachers or student teaching (with ID representing identification).

The entries in each column consist of the cited section ("§") in that state's official statutory compilation and a parenthetical for the abbreviated special feature(s).

For an explanation of these entries on a column by column and, within each column, on a row-by-row basis, please see Chapter II. The pertinent narrative is in the first part of this section.

	Authorization	Definitions	ST Prerequisites	ST Authority	ST Protection	Coop. Tchr.	Other
AL							
AK							
AZ							
AR	§ 6-17-305 (sch. district)				§ 6-17-305(e) (tchr.)		
CA			§ 44320(a) (limits)				§ 44320(d) (ID and health clearance) § 44830.3(a) (special district intern program)
CO	§ 22-62-103(1) (sch. district)	§ 22-62-103 (student tchr. & student tchg.)					
CT							
DE							
FL							
GA		§ 20-2-833(a) (student tchg.)				§ 20-2-833(a) (certificate)	§ 20-2-168 (summer program)
HI							
ID							
IL							105 ILCS 5/10-22.34 (duty limit)
IN							

(continued)

	Authorization	Definitions	ST Prerequisites	ST Authority	ST Protection	Coop. Tchr.	Other
IA	§ 272.27 (written contract)				§ 272.27 (2 protections)	§ 262.75 (incentives & orientation)	§ 272.25 (minimum time and experiences)
KS	§ 72-1392						§ 72-1392 (student teaching licenses)
KY	§ 161.042 (w. state regs)			§ 6-107(c) (certified tchr.)	§ 161.042 (certified tchr.)		§ 161.042 (criminal background check)
LA							
ME							
MD	§ 6-107(a)			§ 6-107)(c) (certified tchr.)		§ 6-107(b) (inservice trg.)	§ 6-107(d) (liability ins. & wrkr. comp.)
MA							
MI			§ 380.1531b (4 areas)			§ 37-132-3 (duty w. regs.)	§ 388.1764e (institutional discrimination)
MN							
MS		§ 37-132-1 (student tchr.)		§ 37-132-3 (certified tchr.)			
MO							
MT							

(continued)

	Authorization	Definitions	ST Prerequisites	ST Authority	ST Protection	Coop. Tchr.	Other
NE		§ 79-875 (student tchr.)		§ 79-875 (certified tchr.)			
NV	§ 396.519						§ 391.096 (substitute teaching)
NH							
NJ					§ 18A:16-6 (2 protections)		
NM							§ 22-10A-6(C) (minimum time)[1]
NY							
NC		§115C-309(a) (student tchr.)			§115C-309(b) (certified tchr.)	§115C-309(c) (duty)	
ND							
OH							
OK							
OR							
PA						24 P.S. § 1864.2 (qualifications & compensation)	
RI							

(continued)

	Authorization	Definitions	ST Prerequisites	ST Authority	ST Protection	Coop. Tchr.	Other
SC	§ 59-26-20(h)						§§ 59-26-20(i) & 59-26-30(B) (specified evaluation and assistance w. regs)
SD							§ 13-10-12 (criminal background check)
TN							
TX							§ 22.0835 (criminal background check)
UT							
VT							
VA							
WA	§ 28A.415.100	§ 28A.415.105 (various terms)				§ 28A.415.105 (qualification)	§§ 28A.415.125 & 28A.415.135 (student teaching centers)
WV	§ 18A-3-1(d) (specified features)			§ 18A-3-1(d) (substitute tchr.)			§ 18A-3-1(e) (nonpublic schools)
WI							
WY							

[1]See also § 22-10A-19.2 (tchr. ed. program accountability reporting of no. of hours).

Appendix B
Case Law Chart

This appendix provides a chronological listing, with key features, of all the published law court decisions on student teaching that are summarized in Chapter III. It can serve as a quick reference to find not only key characteristics within but also—in terms of overall trends—among the cases.

The first column of the table provides the abbreviated name of the decision; the full citation is provided in the reference list. The second column lists the year of the court's decision in the case. The third column lists the jurisdiction, with the official abbreviations of the court. For example, "Cal. S. Ct." refers to the California Supreme Court.

The next three columns show the case role of the student teacher (ST), the institution of higher education (IHE), and the local education agency (LEA), which is the generic descriptor for the school district. The case role entries are in terms of the trial level (even if the case is at the appellate level) as follows: P = plaintiff, D = defendant, and NP = non-party. For the IHE and the LEA, the NP entry only appears for the institution that had the closer connection to the actual defendant. For example, if the student teacher sued the Internal Revenue Service (IRS) based on his employment status with the school district, the NP listing only appears under LEA, not IHE. In one case—*Arrowhead*—the LEA was the effective plaintiff, having started the case with the state administrative agency for labor relations, even though the agency was the named party upon judicial review; thus, the entry in this case was P.

The next four columns, which have the overall heading of "Issues," designate the basis of the court's rulings in terms of (1) Const. = federal constitution, (2) leg./reg. = federal legislation/regulations, (3) state statute, or (4) state common law. If the court decision had a ruling in more than one of these four categories, its listing has more than one row. For example, *Nickerson* (1999) had one ruling on a constitutional issue, specifically Fourteenth Amendment due process, and another on a contractual claim, thus accounting for two rows in the chart. The entries are generally merely Xs, except where clearly differentiable. For example, in the Constitution ("Const.") column, Am. I = First Amendment, and Am XIV = Fourteenth Amendment. Similarly, in the common law column, negl. = negligence, defam. = defamation, and priv. = invasion of privacy.

The winning party column designates the side that won at the highest judicial level that the case reached. ST = student teacher, IHE = institution of higher education, LEA = local education agency, IRS = Internal Revenue Service, private co. = private company. If the decision in favor of the plaintiff student teacher was inconclusive, e.g., denial of the defendant's motion for dismissal or summary judgment, the entry is in brackets with "Inc." added, e.g., [ST-Inc.].

Finally, in place of a separate Table of Cases, the last column provides the page number in Chapter III where the summary for the court's decision starts.

See the "Summary" section of Chapter III for the synthesis of these results with those of the corresponding narratives.

Table B.1 Case Law Chart

Case	Year	Court	Role ST	Role IHE	Role LEA	Const.	Federal Leg./Reg.	State Statute	Common Law	Winning Party	Page No.
Miller	1902	Cal. S. Ct.	P	D		Am. XIV				ST	p. 54
Lindblad	1906	Ill. S. Ct.	NP		D			X		Taxpayer	p. 42
Spedden	1914	W.Va. S. Ct.	NP		D			X		LEA	p. 43
Blanchard	1916	W.Va. S. Ct.	NP		D			X		LEA	p. 43
Clay	1919	Iowa S. Ct.	NP		D			X		LEA	p. 43
Gardner	1939	N.Y. S. Ct.	NP		D				negl.	Parent	p. 40
Robinson	1958	Fla. App.	P	D					contract	IHE	p. 36
Schwerm	1966	Tax Ct.	P		NP		IRS reg.			IRS	p. 65
Reese	1967	Tax Ct.	P		NP		IRS reg.			IRS	p. 64
Scott	1969	M.D. Ala.	P	D		Am. I&XIV				IHE	p. 48
James	1971	S.D. W.Va.	P	D	D	Am. I&XIV				IHE, LEA	p. 36
Rowe	1971	D. Kan.	P		D	Am. XIV				LEA	p. 46
Lai	1971	E.D.N.C.	P	D		Am. XIV				IHE	p. 37
Moore	1973	W.D.N.C.	P		D	Am. I&XIV				ST	p. 60
Abrams	1974	Tax Ct.	P		NP		IRS reg.			IRS	p. 65
Bredahl	1977	Tax Ct.	P		NP		IRS reg.			ST	p. 66
Betts	1978	Mich. S. Ct.	P		D			X		ST	p. 38
Brahatchek	1979	Neb. S. Ct.	NP		D				negl.	ST	p. 41
Aubuchon	1979	E.D. Mo.	P	D		Am. XIV				IHE	p. 55
Hoffman	1983	W.Va. S. Ct	P	D	D	Am. XIV				IHE, LEA	p. 56
Dello	1984	N.Y. App.	P	D					negl.	IHE	p. 38
Arrowhead	1984	Wis. S. Ct.	NP		(P)			X		LEA	p. 44
Arbegast	1985	N.Y. S. Ct.	P		NP				negl.	Private co.	p. 39
Stark	1985	8th Cir.	NP			Am. I				Taxpayers	p. 44
Arko	1987	D. Colo.	P	D		Am. XIV				IHE	p. 61
Embrey	1991	Ohio App.	P	D					contract	IHE	p. 61

Table B.1 (continued)

Case	Year	Court	Role ST	Role IHE	Role LEA	Const.	Issues Federal Leg./Reg.	State Statute	Common Law	Winning Party	Page No.
Lucas	1994	Vt. S. Ct.	P	D		Am. XIV		X		IHE	p. 56
Rust	1994	Mass. App.	P	D					contract, defam.	IHE	p. 62
Banks	1995	Cal. App.	P	D					negl.	IHE	p. 57
Holt	1996	9th Cir.	P	D		Am. I				IHE	p. 33
Everett	1998	11th Cir.	P	D	D		§504/ADA			IHE, LEA	p. 42
Hennessy	1999	1st Cir.	P	D	D	Am. I&XIV				IHE, LEA	p. 58
Nickerson	1999	Alaska S. Ct.	P	D		Am. XIV			contract	IHE [ST-Inc.]	p. 48
Brown	2000	Conn. App.	D		D			X	negl.	LEA, ST	p. 41
Furlong	2001	Mont. Dist. Ct.	P	D					negl., contract	IHE	p. 33
Doe	2001	Wash. S. Ct.	P	D					defam./priv.	ST	p. 47
	2002	S. Ct.	"	"			FERPA			IHE	
Bulloch	2002	Ill. Ct. Cl.	P	D					contract	IHE	p. 62
Swift	2002	E.D. La.	P	D	D	Am. XIV				IHE, LEA	p. 50
			"	"	"				contract	" "	
Hunt	2002	Alaska S. Ct.	P	D		Am. XIV		X		IHE	p. 34
			"	"						"	
Hutchings	2003	6th Cir.	P	D					negl., contract	IHE	p. 63
Cornell	2005	E.D. Tex.	P		D	Am. XIV?				LEA	p. 47
Burns	2007	W.D. Pa.	P	D	D		§504/ADA			[ST-Inc.]	p. 63
Orange County	2007	Fla. App.	P		D			X		LEA	p. 39

Leone	2007	D. Conn.	P	D		Am. XIV	IHE	p. 50
"	"	"	"	"		Am V	"	
Snyder	2008	E. D. Pa.	P	D		Am. I	IHE	p. 52
Miller	2008	M. D. Ala.	P	D	D	Am. I	LEA	p. 53
Thomas	2008	D. Minn.	P	D		ADA	X	IHE	p. 35

P = Plaintiff
D = Defendant
NP = Non-party

ST = Student Teacher
IHE = Institution of Higher Education
LEA = Local Education Agency

[ST-Inc.] = inconclusive win for Student Teacher

Appendix C

Case Scenarios

This appendix provides case scenarios that can serve in preparation for and/or as the culmination of the material in Chapters I and III. As preparation, discussion of one or more of the case scenarios can stimulate interest in and can signal awareness to the variety of legal issues that face the constituencies of student teaching—student teachers, supervising faculty, and cooperating teachers. As culmination, discussion of one or more of the case scenarios can review, apply, and re-check the contents in the primer and case synthesis chapters.

We provide here four case scenarios, each representing a summary of the facts of a court decision summarized in Chapter III. The more complete factual detail and legal conclusions are available in the court's opinion, which is cited in the footnote for the case scenario. A few illustrative discussion questions are at the end of each scenario. The first two case scenarios represent the first two categories of Chapter III—admission/placement of student teachers and conditions of student teaching. The last two represent the most common category of the pertinent litigation to date—dismissal of student teachers.

CASE SCENARIO 1: ADMISSION/PLACEMENT OF STUDENTS TEACHERS[1]

In the fall of 2004, Jenelle Thomas transferred to Hamline University to pursue majors in both music and education as part of the music education certification program. In her Educational Psychology class that term, Thomas began to experience problems. She missed classes, neglected to turn in assignments, and rarely interacted with others in or out of class. When Thomas informed her professor that she suffered from depression, he allowed her extra time to complete assignments. When Thomas still could not finish the required work, she asked for, and was granted, a medical withdrawal so that she could retake the class without negative repercussions. Thomas also had problems in other classes; for example, one of the professors found her to be "negative, unresponsive, reluctant, and almost mildly defiant."

Thomas' academic advisor, Dr. McLane, informally provided her with feedback about the faculty concerns. Thomas admitted she had trouble interacting with people, but her performance did not improve. Following their informal advising session, Dr. McLane sent the following e-mail to Dr. Watson, the chair of the Education Department:

Dwight:

I have serious concerns about Jenelle Thomas pursuing music licensure. Unfortunately we have no academic/content grounds for preventing Jenelle from moving forward. She is quite able to handle the material, quite able to wave her arms as a conductor, she can hear, she's a good pianist and singer, etc. But she's one of the most negative people I've ever encountered. I've talked with Jenelle several times about her suitability for the field and have gotten nowhere. The only institutional barrier I can foresee putting in her path is to fail her from student teaching. That would (I suspect) get very ugly.

In accordance with university procedure, Dr. Watson convened a case conference for the faculty members and Thomas. According to the notes from that conference, the professors pointed out Thomas' areas of strengths and weaknesses, specifying particular concerns about her "interaction with people, ability and willingness to teach music as an expressive art, providing reinforcement and encouragement to students, meeting deadlines, and attendance." Thomas acknowledged these concerns and explained that she suffered from depression. However, she asserted that she was a "different person" while teaching. As an accommodation to her assertion, the faculty members asked her to schedule and teach a lesson that they could observe, demonstrating the proficiency necessary for student teaching.

Subsequent to the meeting, Thomas decided not to do the teaching observation, considering it to be unfair and discriminatory; in her view, she was being set up to fail. At the end of that semester, Thomas' low grades had cumulated to the point of putting her on academic probation. The faculty decided not to allow her to register for student teaching or continue in the certification program because she had not performed the observation alternative and her Fs were in courses central to the music education curriculum. After apparently providing Thomas with notice and, upon her objections based on depression, a formal review, the university finalized the dismissal decision. Thomas promptly filed suit in federal court, claiming that the university discriminated against her in violation of the Americans with Disabilities Act (ADA).

DISCUSSION QUESTIONS

1. Does the ADA apply to Hamline University, which is a private institution of higher education?
2. Assuming for the sake of argument a "yes" answer to question 1, does Thomas have a disability as defined under the ADA?
3. Assuming again for the sake of discussion a "yes" to the previous question, did Hamline fail to provide reasonable accommodations and otherwise discriminate against, i.e., provide disparate treatment to, Thomas on the basis of her disability?

CASE SCENARIO 2: CONDITIONS OF STUDENT TEACHING[2]

Christy Arbegast was a student teacher in South New Berlin School District in New York. She agreed to participate with other school staff members in a fund-raising event—a donkey basketball game—for the senior class. A private company provided the donkeys, helmets for each player, and an employee who transported and handled the animals. The company employee also gave instructions to the participants and acted as referee of the game. In return, as specified in the contract with the district, the company received a percentage of the receipts.

During the preparations immediately before the event, the company employee read a warning to all of the prospective participants that donkeys buck and put their heads down, causing people to fall off, and that participation was at their own risk. In the first of the two games in the event, the faculty team, which included Arbegast, beat a team from the local fire department. Arbegast enjoyed herself without any mishaps. In the subsequent game against the senior class team, however, the company employee assigned Arbegast to a larger and rather fearsome, stubborn donkey. Arbegast spent a good deal of the game walking the donkey around but, at the urging of another faculty member, mounted it. Soon thereafter she was thrown over the donkey's head when it put its head down and suddenly stopped. As a result, Arbegast suffered permanent injury to her left arm.

Arbegast filed suit in state court against both the school district and the private company for compensatory damages. Her two alternate claims were strict liability and negligence, both based on the donkey's vicious propensities. The company's defense was express assumption of the risk and contributory negligence.

DISCUSSION QUESTIONS

1. What would be Arbegast's arguments for her negligence and strict liability claims against the private company? What would the company's defenses to each claim be, depending on the particular variations from one state to another?
2. What additional, overall defense may the school district have, depending on the particular state?
3. What role would insurance coverage probably play for the school district, the company, and the student teacher?

CASE SCENARIO 3: DISMISSAL OF STUDENT TEACHERS[3]

Stacy Snyder was a secondary education major at Millersville University, a public institution of higher education in Pennsylvania. She started her internship at Conestoga Valley High School, where Nicole Reinking served as her cooperating teacher. After spending her first weeks in Reinking's twelfth grade English classes, Snyder started her teaching experience. Within three months, Snyder was teaching a full load of courses. However, she experienced difficulty with respect to her over-familiarity with her students. For example, after conducting observations, the Millersville supervising faculty member, Barry Girvin, noted that she had difficulty maintaining a formal teaching manner. Snyder also exhibited other performance problems. Specifically, Reinking provided her with continuing feedback about not only her inappropriate manner with students but also her grammar mistakes, her inadequate classroom management, and her poor subject matter understanding.

For his part of the mid-semester evaluation, Girvin rated Snyder as satisfactory in most professionalism categories, but as needing improvement in appropriate communication with others—including students, supervisors, and cooperating teachers—and in establishing "proper teacher-student boundaries." For her part of the mid-semester evaluation, Reinking identified several areas needing "significant remediation," including preparation, performance, and student learning. Although agreeing with Girvin that Snyder had made "reasonable progress" in most areas in the professionalism category, Reinking provided an accompanying comment that Snyder's efforts to "share her personal life" with the students crossed into "unprofessionalism."

Contrary to Girvin's warning during the orientation at the outset of student teaching not to post information about her students or her cooperating teacher on her personal webpage, Snyder communicated about personal matters with her students via her MySpace webpage. On several occasions, despite feedback from Reinking not to do so, she informed the students during class that she had a MySpace webpage. Finally, on the fourth month of student teaching, Snyder posted a photo of herself drinking alcohol accompanied by this MySpace message:

> One of my students was on here looking at my page, which is fine. I have nothing to hide. I am over 21, and I don't say anything that will hurt me (in the long run). Plus, I don't think that they would stoop that low as to mess with my future. So, bring on the love! I figure a couple of students will actually send me a message when I am no longer their official teacher. They keep asking me why I won't apply there. Do you think it would hurt me to tell them the real reason (or who the problem was)?.

On the next day, another teacher accessed Snyder's MySpace account and showed the posting to Reinking, who thought the reference in the last line was to her and that in any event the photo and posting were inappropriate. Reinking showed a copy to her supervisor, who considered the posting a blatant act of insubordination. The supervisor contacted the school district superintendent, who in turn barred Snyder from the campus. In an attempt to improve the situation, Snyder wrote an error-filled apology to the cooperating teacher, school administrators, and supervising professor, which asked for forgiveness but sealed her fate. Subsequently, Girvin and Reinking evaluated Snyder's professionalism as unsatisfactory. As a result, Snyder did not graduate with a degree in secondary education; instead the university granted her a B.A. in English. She unsuccessfully appealed to the dean and then to the academic vice president.

Snyder sued the university in federal court, claiming a violation of her First Amendment freedom of expression. The relief that she sought was an injunction ordering the university to award her a degree in secondary education and to take the necessary steps to ensure her state teacher certification.

DISCUSSION QUESTIONS

1. What was the applicable "test," or set of standards, that the court applied to Snyder's First Amendment claim?
2. Applying this test, did Snyder prevail? Why or why not?
3. How would your answer to #2 differ before versus after the Supreme Court's decision in *Garcetti v. Ceballos* (2006)?

CASE SCENARIO 4: DISMISSAL OF STUDENT TEACHERS[4]

In late fall of 1992, John Doe, an elementary education student at a Catholic university, had a sexually intimate relationship with Jane, a student who was studying special education at the same university. In early October 1993, Roberta League, the university's teacher certification specialist, overheard Julia Lynch, a student, talking with another student about her dissatisfaction with the way the school dealt with complaints of date rape. Lynch claimed that she had observed Jane in obvious physical pain, which Jane reported to be the result of having sex with Doe.

Recognizing Doe's name as a student teacher in the education program, League informed Dr. Susan Kyle, university's director of field experience for student teachers, of the information that she had overheard. League and Kyle proceeded to conduct an investigation, which included numerous university personnel. As part of their investigation, Lynch reported a conversation she had with Jane suggesting that Doe had sexually assaulted her three times in late November or December of 1992. Lynch also reported to them that she had accompanied Jane to the student health center soon after the last assault and that the nurse on duty had concluded that Jane had been date raped. Lynch further reported that on the way back from the health center Jane claimed Doe had verbally coerced her into participating in "aberrant sexual behavior" and had urged her to engage in multiple-partner sex.

In late October, Kyle met with Jane and told her about the date rape allegations. According to Kyle, during the meeting, Jane stated: "I guess I don't really know what rape is. . . . I promised Doe I wouldn't tell." However, in answer to Kyle's request, Jane refused to make a formal statement. Jane also talked with Professor Sweeney, who subsequently prepared a written declaration stating that Jane told him the following: (1) Doe had sexually assaulted her on three occasions, each time more violent and abusive; (2) she had screamed and tried to get away; and (3) Doe repeatedly threatened her life, and she did not believe the university could protect her from him. The department chair, who apparently had also spoken with Jane, maintained that she would say that nothing had happened, fearing Doe's anger about discussing their relationship with others.

In February 1994, Corinne McGuigan, the dean of the School of Education, met with League, Kyle, Sweeney, and the department chair. They reported this information to her, whereupon she requested and subsequently received written summaries of what they had told her. After considering the matter, she concluded that there was sufficient evidence of a serious behavioral problem to preclude her from signing the moral character affidavit supporting Doe's application for teacher certification.

On March 4, 1994, which happened to be day he made his final payment of fees and tuition to the university, Doe first learned about the university's investigation of him as a result of a phone call asking him to come to Dean McGuigan's office. Specifically, the office gave him a letter from the dean. The letter explained that, in light of allegations of sexual assault, the dean would not give Doe the moral character affidavit required to support his application for certification to teach. Upon his inquiry, the dean refused to tell Doe who had made the allegations against him. Finally, she told Doe that he had no right to appeal her decision.

Doe sued the university, its administrative officials, and their cited sources of information for various common law torts, including defamation and negligent investigation, and for violating the nondisclosure provision of the Family Educational Rights and Privacy Act (FERPA). At the trial, Jane testified that the declarations of Lynch, Kyle, Sweeney, and the department chair were not true.

DISCUSSION QUESTIONS

1. What are the basic elements, defenses, and likely application of each of these torts in Doe's case—a) invasion of privacy; b) negligence; and c) defamation?
2. Why didn't Doe sue on the basis of Fourteenth Amendment procedural or substantive due process? If such claims would have been possible, what would have been the applicable standards (or precedents) and likely outcome?
3. What was the ultimate disposition of Doe's FERPA claim? What is the effect of this ruling, including the means of recourse for victims of FERPA violations?

Appendix D

Glossary[1]

ADA The Americans with Disabilities Act – federal legislation and accompanying detailed regulations that prohibit disability discrimination in "public entities," including public schools, and "private places of public accommodations," including private schools and colleges/universities

ADEA The Age Discrimination in Employment Act – the federal statute that prohibits discrimination based on age in the employment context for persons at least 40 years old and that the EEOC administers

certiorari A written request for appellate review, typically to the Supreme Court, which has the discretion either to deny or to grant it

circuit court Within the federal judiciary, this term, which is a shorthand for "Circuit Court of Appeals," refers to the intermediate, appellate court, whereas in the various state judicial systems it may be the name of a trial or appellate level court

common law Judge-made law – strictly speaking, case law based on previous case law without the framework of statutes or regulations

compensatory damages Monetary relief that a court awards to "make whole" the plaintiff for the physical and emotional injuries resulting from a civil law violation

construction A synonym in the legal context for interpretation, usually used in reference to courts determining the intent of legislation based on its language, legislative history, and—sometimes—general principles called "canons of construction"

defamation The tort of harming another person's reputation by "publication" (i.e., dissemination to at least one third party) of untruthful statements of purported fact – in its oral form called "slander" and in its written form called "libel"

deference The doctrine or institutional tradition of presuming, subject to rebuttal, that the decision of another individual or organization is correct, thus affording it the latitude of the benefit of the doubt – often associated with a court deferring to the decision of an administrative agency, such as a school board or its administrators

dicta Statements in the court's opinion that are not essential to its decision and, thus, are not part of the holding, or rule, of the case

dismissal A pre-trial decision in favor of the defendant, upon its request, because even upon accepting the plaintiff's allegations as facts, the law does not support the claims

district court Within the federal judiciary, this name refers to the trial court, whereas within the various state judiciaries it may refer to the trial or another level

EAA The Equal Access Act – federal legislation that applies to secondary schools that receive federal financial assistance and that requires them to treat all "noncurriculum-related" student groups equally, i.e., either deny or—except for those who would cause substantial disruption—grant official recognition and facilities use to all such groups

EEOC The Equal Employment Opportunities Commission – the federal agency that administers various civil rights statutes in the employment context

EPA The Equal Pay Act – federal legislation that prohibits sex discrimination in employment compensation among employers, including public and private schools, that have at least 20 employees

exhaustion General judicial principle, with exceptions, that the plaintiff, or complainant, should use available administrative remedies before resorting to litigation in court

fair use The judicial doctrine codified in the federal Copyright Act that provides a limited exception for not-for-profit educational institutions to use multiple copies of a work based on criteria for brevity, spontaneity, and cumulative effect

FERPA The Family Educational Rights and Privacy Act – federal legislation that, along with its regulations, specifies rights for the parent (until the student reaches age 18, whereupon they transfer to the student) of access and nondisclosure of the student's educational records in institutions that receive federal funds – administered by FPCO

FMLA The Family and Medical Leave Act of 1993– federal legislation that requires employers with more than 50 employees to grant eligible employees up to 12 workweeks of unpaid leave within a 12-month period for

Glossary 95

specified reasons, such as the birth and care of said employee's newborn child or to care for a family member with a serious health condition

FPCO The Family Policy Compliance Office – part of the U.S. Department of Education that administers federal parent-student privacy laws, such as FERPA

First Amendment freedom of expression "Congress shall make no law . . . abridging the freedom of speech."

First Amendment religion (Establishment and Free Exercise) clauses "Congress shall make no law respecting an establishment of religion, or prohibiting the free exercise thereof."

Fourth Amendment "The right of the people to be secure in their persons, houses, papers, and effects, against unreasonable searches and seizures, shall not be violated, and no warrants shall issue, but upon probable cause, supported by oath or affirmation, and particularly describing the place to be searched, and the persons or things to be seized."

Fourteenth Amendment due process clause "[N]or shall any State deprive any person of life, liberty, or property, without due process of law."

Fourteenth Amendment equal protection clause "[Nor shall any State] deny to any person within its jurisdiction the equal protection of the laws."

HIPAA The Health Insurance Portability and Accountability Act – federal legislation originally enacted in 1996 that not only protects employees' health insurance upon losing or changing jobs but has specific rules for the security and privacy of their health data

IDEA The Individuals with Disabilities Education Act – federal funding legislation that is summarized in Chapter I of this volume

legislative history The recorded proceedings of the committees and on the floor of the chambers of Congress or a state legislature that provides for such transcriptions

NCLB The No Child Left Behind Act of 2001 – omnibus federal legislation applicable in K–12 education that is summarized in Part II of this volume

OCR The Office for Civil Rights – the agency within the U.S. Department of Education that administers various federal civil rights statutes, including the respective regulations, that apply to K–12 and postsecondary students, such as § 504 and Title IX

PDA The Pregnancy Discrimination Act of 1978 – amendments to Title VII to expressly include within sex discrimination in employment "because of or on the basis of pregnancy, childbirth, or related medical conditions"

PPRA The Protection of Pupil Rights Amendment – provides parents with the right to inspect materials connected with federally funded surveys, analyses, or evaluations and requires their written permission for their minor children's participation for such federally funded activities that reveal specified forms of information (e.g., "sex behavior and attitudes") – enforced by FPCO

plaintiff The party that initiates the suit at the trial level (against one or more "defendants")

pro se "For oneself"; proceeding as a litigant in court without attorney representation

punitive damages Also known as "exemplary damages," this form of judicial remedy is for exceptional cases where the defendant's conduct was malicious, or criminal-like, thus warranting extra monetary relief beyond compensatory damages

reporter In the context of law, a set of volumes that contains court decisions for a given level of the judiciary, region of the country, or specialized subject area

respondeat superior "Let the master answer"; attaching liability for the acts of an employee, within the scope of employment, to the employer

§ The symbol for "Section," which is the part of legislation or regulation typically referred to rather than the page number (because it may either be a small part of a page or conversely consist of several pages)

§ **504** Federal legislation, with accompanying regulations, that prohibits disability discrimination in institutions receiving federal financial assistance – applies, along with the ADA, to students, employees, and other individuals

stare decisis The short form of *stare decisis et quieta non movere* ("to stand by and adhere to decisions and not disturb what is settled") – the legal principle that obligates judges to follow the precedents established in prior decisions

summary judgment A decision without a trial based on the court's determination that there is no major factual issue in dispute and, thus, upon proper motion from either party, that the court may summarily reach resolution as a matter of law.

Tenth Amendment "The powers not delegated to the United States by the Constitution, nor prohibited by it to the States, are reserved to the States."

Title I Title I of the Elementary and Secondary Education Act of 1965 – federal funding legislation, now part of the NCLB, that supports compensatory (e.g., reading) services from preschool through high school to educational institutions, primarily public elementary schools, with a high percentage of students from low-income families

Title VI Title VI of the Civil Rights Act of 1964 – federal legislation, with accompanying regulations, prohibiting discrimination "on the basis of race, color, or national origin" (of students) in educational institutions that receive federal financial assistance

Title VII Title VII of the Civil Rights Act of 1964, also known as the Equal Employment Opportunities Act – federal legislation, along with regulations, prohibiting employment discrimination based on race, color, national origin, gender, or religion by employers with 15 or more employees

Title IX Title IX of the Education Amendments of 1972 – federal legislation prohibiting discrimination based on gender in programs or activities receiving federal financial assistance

tort A civil wrong, which is judicially remediable under each state's common law, that is not covered by contract

ultra vires Beyond the scope of authority

viewpoint discrimination The doctrine under First Amendment freedom of expression that prohibits governmental content-based restrictions based on the viewpoint expressed

Appendix E

Useful Resources: A Sampler[1]

BOOKS:

Beckham, J., & Dagley, D. (2005). *Contemporary issues in higher education law.* Dayton, OH: Education Law Association.

Cambron-McCabe, N. H., McCarthy, M. M., & Thomas, S. B. (2009). *Legal rights of teachers and students.* Boston: Pearson.

Fischer, L., Schimmel, D., & Stellman, L. R. (2006). *Teachers and the law.* Boston: Pearson.

Imber, M., & van Geel, T. (2004). *A teacher's guide to education law.* New York, NY: Routledge.

Kaplin, W. A., & Lee, B. A. (2006). *The law of higher education.* San Francisco: Jossey-Bass.

Manos, M. A. (2007). *Knowing where to draw the line: Ethical and legal standards for best classroom practice.* Lanham, MD: Rowman & Littlefield.

Olivas, M. (2006). *The law of higher education: Cases and materials on colleges in court.* Durham, NC: Carolina Press.

Russo, C. (Ed.) (in press). *Encyclopedia of higher education law.* Thousand Oaks, CA: Sage.

Smith, M. H. (2005). *The legal, professional, and ethical dimensions of higher education.* Philadelphia, PA: Lippincott, Williams & Wilkins.

Thomas, S. B., Cambron-McCabe, M. H., & McCarthy, M. M. (2009). *Public school law: Teachers' and students' rights.* Boston: Pearson.

Zirkel, P. A. (in press). *A digest of Supreme Court decisions affecting education.* Dayton, OH: Education Law Association.

Appendix E

JOURNALS:

Action in Teacher Education (Association of Teacher Educators) — Summer 2008 issue (v. 30, no. 2) on "teacher education and the law"
BYU Journal of Education and Law (Brigham Young University School of Law).
Journal of College and University Law (University of Notre Dame School of Law).
Journal of Law and Education (University of South Carolina School of Law).
West's Education Law Reporter (West Publishing Co.)[2]

ORGANIZATIONS:

Education Law Association. www.educationlaw.org.
National Council of College and University Attorneys. www.nacua.org.

WEBSITE MATERIALS:

Bathon, J. M. (n.d.). The Edjurist (a blog site as well as search engine on education law issues). http://www.edjurist.com/find-ed-law-info/.
Becker, J., & Bathon, J. M. (n.d.) NASSP online school law guide. http://www.principals.org/s_nassp/sec_inside.asp?CID=1632&DID=58566.
Cornell University Law School. (n.d.). Legal information institute (free database for legal research). http://www4.law.cornell.edu/.
Educational Cyber Playground. (n.d.). K–12 copyright laws: Primer for teachers. http://www.edu-cyberpg.com/Teachers/copyrightlaw.html.
Haynes, C. C., & Thomas, O. (2007). A teacher's guide to religion in the schools. In *Finding common ground.* http://www.firstamendmentcenter.org/about.aspx?id=6276.
National School Boards Association. (n.d.). Legal clips (weekly update). http://www.nsba.org/MainMenu/SchoolLaw/LegalClips.aspx.
School Leaders Risk Management Association (n.d.). Education Risk Management Dateline (monthly brief update of major court decisions in education). http://www.slrma.org/calendarofevents.aspx
Starr, L. (2004). The educator's guide to copyright and fair use. http://www.educationworld.com/a_curr/curr280.shtml.
United States Department of Education (n.d.). Building the legacy: IDEA 2004. http://idea.ed.gov/.
University of Texas School of Law (n.d.). Education law-specific resources. http://tarlton.law.utexas.edu/vlibrary/subject/education/education.html.
Weiman, H. (2007). Ed Psyc Central Psychoeducational Resource Center. http://edpsyccentral.org/ - "laws, regs, standards & ethics".

Notes

CHAPTER 1

1. Other sources—e.g., the Lexis and Westlaw electronic databases—contain unpublished court decisions in addition to those that are officially published (i.e., submitted by the court and selected by the duly designated official publication).

2. The definition of disability under Section 504 and the ADA, which is generally broader than that under the IDEA, has three alternative prongs in relation to the individual at issue: (1) a physical or mental impairment that substantially limits a major life activity; (2) a record of such an impairment; or (3) regarded as having such an impairment."

3. See the Glossary at the end of this volume for the full list and explanation of the acronyms and abbreviations.

4. Some states have the traditional form of contributory negligence, where the plaintiff's negligence serves as an absolute defense, or complete bar to recovery of damages. Other states have adopted by case law or statute pure or modified comparative negligence, which reduce but do not necessarily eliminate the defendant's liability for negligence. Under both forms of comparative negligence, the jury determines whether each side was negligent and, if so, the relative percentages. In the pure form, the total amount of damages is reduced by the plaintiff's percentage. In the modified form, the reduction is proportional up to 50%, but thereafter (i.e., the plaintiff's percentage was more than the defendant's percentage), the plaintiff receives nothing.

CHAPTER 2

1. A separate Georgia law requires each district to have this program for students who failed one or more subjects or who were retained in grade. GA. CODE ANN., § 20-2-168 (2008).

CHAPTER 3

1. For those unpublished decisions that were available in both databases, we listed in the References only the Westlaw citation, which is designated with "WL," for the sake of brevity and uniformity.

2. The asterisk before a cited page number designates that the court decision is only available on an electronic database, thus signifying its sequence in this not formally, or traditionally, published format.

3. Although this internship could only be marginally considered student teaching, we included this case—and the next one, which was for a regular teaching role but in the postsecondary context—only to complete the limited line of authority in the income tax context.

APPENDIX C

1. Thomas v. Hamline, 2008 U.S. Dist. LEXIS 94873 (D. Minn. 2008).
2. Arbegast v. Bd. of Educ., 480 N.E.2d 365 (N.Y. 1985).
3. Snyder v. Millersville Univ., 2009 WL 5093140 (E. D. Pa. 2009).
4. Doe v. Gonzaga Univ., 24 P.3d 390 (Wash. 2001), *rev'd on FERPA grounds sub nom. Gonzaga Univ. v. Doe*, 536 U.S. 273 (2002).

APPENDIX D

1. This glossary is generic such that it includes not only the legal terms but also abbreviations and acronyms in this volume.

APPENDIX E

1. This list is a representative sample of relatively recent legal sources that are specific to the overlapping areas that have student teaching at the intersection: (1) K-12 teachers and students, and (2) in the absence of books specific to higher education students or teachers, higher education law overall. Thus, the "Books" section does not include the many texts and other books concerning school law in general or special education in particular. Due to their relative scarcity, the "Journals" and "Organizations" sections are broader but still do not include those that are not specific to law. Conversely, due to its more extensive variety, the "Website" section excludes the several nongovernmental sites specific to special education (e.g., wrightslaw.com).

2. This specialized source is a hybrid, being a "reporter" (as defined in the Glossary) of court decisions in the education context and also a periodical for articles specific to education law.

Index

Abrams v. Commissioner of Internal Revenue, 65, 81
administrative law, 14–15
Age Discrimination in Employment Act, 16, 93
Alabama
    freedom of expression (First Amendment) federal case, 53
    procedural due process (Fourteenth Amendment) federal case, 48
Alaska
    prerequisite for placement case, 34–35
    suspension or dismissal from placement, 48–50
Americans with Disabilities Act, 5, 14–16, 35, 42, 63–64, 68, 87, 93, 101
Arbegast v. Board of Education, 39, 81, 87–88
Arizona, statutory prerequisites for student teaching, 75
Arkansas
    enabling legislation, 25, 75
    statutory immunity of student teachers, 26, 75
Arko v. U.S. Air Force Reserve Officer Training, 61, 81

Arrowhead United Teachers Organization v. Wisconsin Employment Relations Commission, 44, 81
attorneys' fees, 34–35, 57–58, 67
Aubuchon v. Olsen, 55, 81

Banks v. Dominican College, 57, 82
Betts v. Ann Arbor Public Schools, 38, 67, 81
Blanchard v. Keppel, 43, 81
Board of Curators of University of Missouri v. Horowitz, 13, 55
Board of Regents v. Roth, 12
Brahatchek v. Millard School District, 41, 81
Bredahl v. Commissioner of Internal Revenue, 66, 81
Brown v. Acorn Acres Inc., 41, 82
Brown v. Board of Education, 14
Bulloch v. State, 62–63, 82
Burns v. Slippery Rock University, 63–64, 82

California
    delegation of power to local entities, 43

California (*Continued*)
  dismissal from student teaching, 54, 57
  statutory prerequisites for student teaching, 26
  statutory special programs for student teachers, 27
certiorari, 8, 93
child abuse, reporting requirements, 20
Children's Internet Protection Act of 2000, 18
circuit court, 6–7, 93
citations to court reporters, 7
Civil Rights Act of 1871, Section 1983, 16
Civil Rights Act of 1964, 97
civil rights law, 16;
  disabilities, 14–15, 35, 42, 63–64, 68, 85–87, 101
  race discrimination (Title VI), 5, 96
  sex discrimination (Title IX), 2, 5, 16, 63
Clay v. Independent School District, 43, 81
collective bargaining and student teachers, 44
Colorado
  enabling legislation, 75
  procedural due process (Fourteenth Amendment) federal case, 61
  statutory definition of student teaching, 75
common law, 19, 22, 38–39, 47, 51, 67, 93
compensatory damages, 21, 47, 54, 88, 93
conduct, 1, 46–48, 51–52, 88–90, 90–91
Connecticut
  negligence by supervising teacher, 41
  procedural due process (Fourteenth Amendment) federal case, 51
constitutional law, 4
  enumerated powers, 3, 96
  equal protection (Fourteenth Amendment), 4, 13–14, 34, 95
  freedom of expression (First Amendment), 8–10, 33, 36–37, 48, 52–54, 60–61, 63, 89–90, 95
  privacy, invasion of (Fourth Amendment), 11–12, 91
  procedural due process (Fourteenth Amendment), 12, 36–38, 46, 48–51, 55–56, 59–61, 91, 95
  religion (establishment clause), 10–11, 44–45, 60
  religion (First Amendment), 3, 10–11, 24, 36, 58, 95
  search and seizure (Fourth Amendment), 11, 95
  supremacy clause, 5
  viewpoint discrimination (First Amendment), 9–11, 97
construction, 8, 93
contracts, 22, 34, 36, 50
Copyright Act of 1976, 18
Cornell v. Pleasant Grove Independent School District, 47–48, 82
courts
  interpretation of statutes, 15
  jurisdiction and hierarchy, 5–7
criminal law, 23

date rape. *See* Conduct
defamation, tort of, 22, 46–47, 47, 57, 62, 91, 93
deference, 23–24, 34, 49, 55, 62–63, 67, 94
Dello v. State, 38, 81
depression. *See* Civil rights law, disabilities
dicta, 44, 46, 50, 54, 56, 94
disabilities. *See* Civil rights law, disabilities
discrimination. *See* Civil rights law; constitutional law, equal protection

dismissal, court, 34, 36, 39, 42, 48, 62, 94
district court, 6–7, 94
Doe v. Gonzaga University, 16, 47, 67, 82, 90–91

Educational Amendments of 1972, 97
educational malpractice, 22, 63
Embrey v. Central State University, 61, 81
enumerated powers. *See* constitutional law, enumerated powers
Equal Access Act, 16, 94
Equal Employment Opportunities Act, 97
Equal Employment Opportunities Commission, 94
Equal Pay Act, 16, 94
equal protection. *See* constitutional law, equal protection
ethics, relationship to law, 2–3
Everett v. Cobb County School District, 42, 82
exhaustion, 15, 51, 56, 68, 94

fair use, 19, 94
Family and Medical Leave Act of 1993, 16, 94
Family Educational Rights and Privacy Act, 16, 47, 91, 94
Family Policy Compliance Office, 95
federalism
    division of power to federal and state governments, 3, 14
    relationship of parts of legal system, 4
Florida
    religion (First Amendment) case, 36
    worker's compensation case, 39–40
freedom of expression. *See* constitutional law, freedom of expression
Furlong v. Carroll College, 33, 82

Garcetti v. Ceballos, 9, 90
Gardner v. State, 40, 81
Georgia
    cooperating teacher statutory requirements, 27, 75
    statutory definition of student teaching, 26, 75
    statutory special programs for student teachers, 27, 75
Gonzaga University v. Doe. *See Doe v. Gonzaga University*
Goss v. Lopez, 12

Health Insurance Portability and Accountability Act, 16, 95
Healy v. James. *See James v. West Virginia Board of Regents*
Hennessey v. City of Melrose, 58, 82
Hoffman v. Grove, 56, 81
Holt v. Munitz, 33, 82
Hunt v. University of Alaska, 34–35, 82
Hutchings v. Vanderbilt University, 63, 82

Illinois
    contract, breach of, 62
    delegation of power to local entities, 42–43
immorality. *See* Conduct
immunity. *See* individual states; State law
incompetence. *See* Student teachers
Indiana, 75
Individuals with Disabilities Education Act, 17, 95, 101
injuries. *See* negligence, tort of; Worker's compensation
intentional torts. *See* torts
Iowa
    cooperating teacher statutory requirements, 76
    delegation of power to local entities, 44

Iowa (*Continued*)
  enabling legislation, 76
  provisional certificates to student teachers, 43
  statutory evaluation of student teachers, 28
  statutory immunity of student teachers, 27, 76
  supervisors and teachers, statutory duties, 27

James v. West Virginia Board of Regents, 9, 36, 81

Kansas
  enabling legislation, 76
  procedural due process (Fourteenth Amendment) case, 46
  statutory student teaching licenses, 28, 76
Kentucky
  criminal background clearance, 76
  enabling legislation, 76
  statutory authority of student teachers, 26, 76
  statutory immunity of student teachers, 26, 76
Ku Klux Klan Act, 16

Lai v. Board of Trustees of East Carolina University, 37, 81
Lee v. Weisman, 10
legislative history, 15, 95
Leone v. Whitford, 51, 83
Lindblad v. Board of Education, 42, 81
Louisiana, procedural due process (Fourteenth Amendment) federal case, 50
Lucas v. Hahn, 56, 82

Maryland
  cooperating teacher statutory requirements, 76
  enabling legislation, 76
  statutory authority of student teachers, 26, 76
  statutory insurance provisions for student teachers, 28, 76
Massachusetts
  contract, breach of, 61
  defamation, tort of, 62
  procedural due process (Fourteenth Amendment) federal case, 58
  religion (establishment clause) federal case, 58
Michigan, 76;
  cooperating teacher statutory requirements, 76
  role as student or employee case, 37–38
  statutory charter schools and student teaching, 28
  statutory prerequisites for student teaching, 26, 76
Miller v. Dailey, 54, 81
Miller v. Houston County Board of Education, 53, 83
Minnesota, federal civil rights case, 35–36
Minnesota Human Rights Act, 35
Mississippi
  statutory authority of student teachers, 26, 76
  statutory definition of student teaching, 76
Missouri, procedural due process (Fourteenth Amendment) federal case, 55
Montana, prerequisite for placement case, 33–34
Moore v. Gaston County Board of Education, 60, 81
moral character. *See* Conduct
Morse v. Frederick, 9

Nebraska
  negligence by supervising teacher, 41

statutory authority of student
teachers, 26, 77
statutory definition of student
teaching, 77
supervisors and teachers, statutory
duties, 27
negligence, tort of, 22, 34, 38–41, 63,
87–88, 91, 101
Nevada
enabling legislation, 77
statutory substitute teaching by
student teachers, 28, 77
New Jersey, statutory immunity of
student teachers, 27, 77
New Mexico, 77
New York, negligence case in, 38–40
Nickerson v. University of Alaska, 32,
48–50, 82
No Child Left Behind Act, 17–18, 95–96
North Carolina
cooperating teacher statutory
requirements, 77
freedom of expression (First
Amendment) federal case, 60
procedural due process (Fourteenth
Amendment), 37–38
statutory definition of student
teaching, 77
statutory immunity of student
teachers, 26, 77
notice and hearings. *See* constitutional
law, procedural due process

Office for Civil Rights, 14, 95
Ohio, breach of contract, 61
*Orange County School Board v.
Powers*, 39, 82

Pennsylvania
cooperating teacher statutory
requirements, 27, 77
disability case in federal court, 63
procedural due process (Fourteenth
Amendment) federal case, 52

Perry v. Sindermann, 12
placement, denial of, 33–35, 48–50
plaintiff, 8, 96
Pregnancy Discrimination Act of 1978,
16, 95
privacy, invasion of. *See* constitutional
law
pro se, 96
pro se suits, 33–34, 47, 61, 68
Protection of Pupil Rights Amendment,
16, 21, 95
public and private institutions, 8, 67
punitive damages, 47, 54, 96

*Reese v. Commissioner of Internal
Revenue*, 64, 66, 81
*Regents of University of Michigan v.
Ewing*, 13
Rehabilitation Act of 1973, 14–15
religion and law. *See* constitutional law
reporter, 7, 96
research method, 32
respondeat superior, 41, 96
Robinson v. University of Miami, 36, 81
Rowe v. Chandler, 46, 60–61, 81
Rust v. Tufts University, 62, 82

*Safford Unified School District #1 v.
Redding*, 11
sanctions, 2
*Schwerm v. Commissioner of Internal
Revenue*, 65, 81
*Scott v. Alabama State Board of
Education*, 32, 48, 81
search and seizure. *See* constitutional
law
Snyder v. Millersville University, 52–53,
83, 88–90
South Carolina
enabling legislation, 78
statutory evaluation of student
teachers, 28, 78
South Dakota, criminal background
clearance, 78

special education, 17, 24
Spedden v. Board of Education, 43, 81
stare decisis, 6, 21, 96
Stark v. St. Cloud State University, 44, 81
state law
    delegation of power to local entities, 3, 5, 19, 42–43
    enabling legislation, 25
    immunity comparable to certified teachers, 26–27
    statutory definition of student teaching, 26
    student teacher authority, 26
student teachers
    collective bargaining and, 44
    criminal background clearance, 20
    delegation of power to local entities, 42–43
    federal statutes and, 15–16
    incompetence, 54–59
    prerequisites, court cases involving, 33–36
    provisional certificates, 43
    role as student or employee, ix, xi, 9, 33, 38, 39–40, 50, 53, 58, 68
    statutory authority granted by states, 26
    statutory definition of student teaching, 26
    statutory prerequisites, 26
    statutory student teaching licenses in Kansas, 28
    success of lawsuits, 67
    suspension or dismissal from placement, 48–50
summary judgment, 34–35, 51, 54, 56–58, 63, 96
supervisors and teachers
    delegation of power to local entities, 42–43
    federal statutes and, 15–16
    licensure, 2–3
    negligence by supervising teacher, 40–41
    state statutes and, 20, 27, 75–78
Swift v. Siesel, 50, 61, 82

taxation of stipend, 64–66
teacher immorality. *See* Conduct
Technology, Education, and Copyright Harmonization Act of 2001, 18
Tennessee, educational malpractice claim in federal court, 63
Tenth Amendment. *See* constitutional law, enumerated powers
Texas
    criminal background clearance, 78
    defamation case in federal court, 46
Thomas v. Hamline University, 35, 83, 85–87
Title I. *See* No Child Left Behind Act
Title VI. *See* civil rights law, race discrimination
Title VII. *See* Civil Rights Act of 1964
Title IX. *See* Educational Amendments of 1972
torts, 21, 97

ultra vires, 4, 97
United States v. American Library Association, Inc., 19
U.S. Department of Education, 5

Vermont, procedural due process (Fourteenth Amendment) case, 56
Vermont Access to Public Records Act, 56–57
viewpoint discrimination. *See* constitutional law, viewpoint discrimination

Washington State
    cooperating teacher statutory requirements, 78
    defamation, tort of, 46–47
    enabling legislation, 78
    statute providing for a network of student teaching centers, 28, 78

statutory definition of student
    teaching, 77
West Virginia
    delegation of power to local entities,
        43
    enabling legislation, 25, 78
    freedom of expression (First
        Amendment), 36–37
    procedural due process (Fourteenth
        Amendment), 36–37, 56

statutory authority of student
    teachers, 26, 78
statutory permission for student
    teachers in non-public schools,
    28, 78
Wisconsin, role as student or employee,
    44
worker's compensation, 20, 38–40

About the Authors

Perry A. Zirkel started his career as teacher in New York City after completing his student teaching at R. L. Thomas High School in Rochester, New York. He co-authored this work during the spring semester of 2009, when he served as the Robinson Scholar in Educational Policy at the University of North Florida while on sabbatical from his position as university professor of education and law at Lehigh University. He has been at Lehigh for more than 30 years, having served as dean of the College of Education and Iacocca Chair of Education, each for five-year periods. He has a Ph.D. in Educational Administration and a J.D. from the University of Connecticut and a Master of Laws degree from Yale University. He has written more than 1,200 publications on various aspects of school law, including the two-volume reference *Section 504, the ADA in the Schools* and regular columns for *Phi Delta Kappan*, *Principal* magazine and *Teaching Exceptional Children*. Past president of the Education Law Association, he has served in various part-time impartial adjudicative roles, including co-chair of Pennsylvania's special education appeals panel from 1990 to 2006. He was the editor for the law-themed summer 2009 issue of *Action in Teacher Education*.

Zorka Karanxha started her career as a teacher in Raqi Qirinxhi High School in Albania. She is an assistant professor in the Department of Educational Leadership and Policy Studies at the University of South Florida. She has an Ed. D. in Educational Leadership from Lehigh University. Her research interests include charter schools, parent involvement, and education law. She has co-authored publications on legal issues of student teachers in *2008 ATE Yearbook*, the 2009 summer issue of *Action in Teacher Education*, and *Sage Encyclopedia of Law and Higher Education*.

www.ingramcontent.com/pod-product-compliance
Lightning Source LLC
Chambersburg PA
CBHW031713230426
43668CB00006B/199